ABENAKI INDIAN
LEGENDS, GRAMMAR AND PLACE NAMES

CONTENTS

———

HENRY LORNE MASTA
Abenaki Ex Past Head Chief

Abenaki Indian Legends, Grammar and Place Names

BY

HENRY LORNE MASTA

Odanak, P. Q.

1932

Editor

La Voix des Bois-Francs.
Victoriaville, P. Q.

REPRINTED 2008,
GLOBAL LANGUAGE PRESS,
TORONTO

Global Language Press
238-1170 Bay St
Toronto ON M5S 2B4
CANADA

http://language-press.com

1-897367-18-X

Printed in the United States of America

FOREWORD

———

This little book lay dormant in the author's mind long before
it was written. Other duties and interests kept thrusting the actual
writing of it aside, so that pen was not set to paper until the winter
of 1929. This was in the 77th year of the author's life. Once started,
it was carried to completion without advice or assistance from
anyone except for a few suggestions made by Prof. E. P. Kelly of
Darmouth and the undersigned. when it was practically finished. In
both form and content it reflects the life long interest of Mr. Masta
in his native tongue, a linguistic conciousness manifestly unusual
in one whose forebears of even two centuries ago were still living
the untutored life of other American aborigines of that period. The
book thus embodies the virtues of a keen and active linguistic
heritage. It can hardly be judged by the rigid canons of academic
criticism, since the author does not pretend that he has presented
a complete philological treatise, in the narrow sense. In my opinion,
the intrinsic interest of the book lies in the virtues of its defects.
The mind of the author is deeply immersed in the idiom which he
sets forth, a relation impossible to the outsider, no matter how well
trained in comparative linguistics.

Henry Lorne Masta was born on March 9th, 1853. He received
his primary and secondary education on the Reserve, and later
attended Sabrevois College, near St-Johns, P. Q. While there he received instruction in Latin for two years and in Greek, one year.
These are the only studies he pursued which may in any sence be
termed philological. But in addition to speaking his native language
with distinction he has achieved fluency in both French and English. For 31 years he occupied the post of schoolmaster in the Pro-
testant school at Odanak and attempted to introduce the children
whom he taught to the grammatical rules governing their language.
Mr. Masta was also chief of his tribe for 20 years and his counsel,
I may add, has always been sought upon matters of importance.

At present the St-Francis Abenaki occupy a small tract of land on the eastern bank of the St-Francis River, about 6 miles from where it joins the St-Lawrence. The language which is native to them belongs to that family of American Indian languages known as Algonkian. Dialecticaly it is very close to that formerly spoken by the Wawenock, the remnants of which still reside at Becancour, P. Q., and to Penobscot, spoken by the Indians of Old Town, Me. These dialects, together with those spoken by the more remotely related Malecite, Passamaquoddy and Micmac and, at an earlier period, by such New England peoples as the Pigwacket, Sakoki, Aroosaguntacook, Norridgewock and Pennacook, all belong to a single linguistic sub-group of the Algonkian stock. Collectively, these peoples have long been known as the Wabanaki. Having allied themselves with the French rather than the English in the Colonial wars of the late 17th century, the remnants of a number of the last named groups, in particular, fled to Canada where missions had been established by French priests. The descendants of these Indians are those which reside at St-Francis (Odanak) and Becancour, to-day.

Father Sebastian Rale, while ministering to the Norridgewock Indians, began to compile a dictionary of their language in 1691. Since a large contingent of this band later migrated to St-Francis, it may be considered the earliest attempt to set down the lexical characteristics of a dialect practically identical with that spoken subsequently in Canada. This dictionary was edited by John Pickering and published in 1833 in a Memoir of the American Academy of Science and Art. F. S. Dickson was preparing another edition of it at the time of his death a few years ago.

Early in the 18th century Father Joseph Aubery, *curé* of the St- Francis Indians also compiled an extensive dictionary which has never been printed. In 1830, P. P. Wz8khilain, the uncle of H. L. Masta, published a primer of his native tongue to set it down in writing. Wz8khilain also made a translation of the Ten Commandments and other Biblical passages which he had printed the same year and later there appeared his Abenaki rendering of the Gospel

of St-Mark. In 1884 the late Chief Joseph Laurent published his
"New Familiar Abenakis and English Dialogues" which contains
a large amount of valuable lexical material.

In addition to the linguistic information recorded by the
priests, mentioned above, and the two Abenaki men referred to,
a discussion of certain espects of this dialect appears in the work
of such scholars as J. D. Prince, F. G. Speck, F. S. Dickson and the
writer.

Finally, a few remarks upon the orthography used by Mr.
Masta seem desirable. While the phonetic symbols used are not
refined to the extent demanded in academic circles, a reasonable
degree of systematization has been achieved. The surd "l" is represented by the combination "hl", the acricative medial surd by "ch"
and the corresponding sonant by "j" (inclining toward the positions
"ts" and "dz", respectively); "w" preceding or following a consonant is equivalent to "u" pronounced as "oo" in English, moon,
the difference being that in Abenaki this sound is uttered with
even a more marqed lip protrustion and weak breath. In consonant
clusters (sonand-surd, "zt", "zs", surdonant, "tb", "sm"; sonant-
sonant, "jb", "db"; surd-surd, "kp" and similar combinations abound-
ign in Mr. Masta's texts) confusion is removed when we know
that they are to be pronounced as independent sounds with a
slight hiatus between them. For the nasalized vowels and the pala-
tal nasal, like "ng" of English "sing", 8 is used. Although the vowels
are not clearly distinguished, "i" at the end of a word may be said
to indicate a long closed vowel like English "ee" while the letter
"e" usually approximates "u" in English "but"; "a" in pronunciation
ranges from "a" in "father" to "a" in English "bat". The combination "ua" is close to the semi-vowel "w" and "h" indicates rough
breathing. Since no accents are indicated it may help the reader
to know that final syllables in Abenaki receive the word accent. The
dieresis (French, "trema") is employed in the conventional manner.

"Strong and weak" in Mr. Masta's terminology are grammatical categories which are the equivalent of animate and inani-

mate as used by other writers on Algonkian languages.

While the language which Mr. Masta expounds is still spoken by many of the Indians of his tribe to-day, French is even more widely used and English is likewise spoken by a large number of individuals. It is inevitable that in another generation there will be still fewer speakers of the St-Francis Abenaki language so that this little book, as time goes on, will embody the crystallization of this native American tongue by one whose generation marks the passing of the period when it still retained a great deal of its aboriginal vigor.

A. Irving Hallawell,

Department of Anthropology,

University of Pennsylvania,

Phila., Pa., U. S. A.

PREFACE

——

It is wonderful how the untutored Abenaki Indians, men, women and children of St-Francis Reserve, Odanak, P. Q. can use grammatical expressions. They unconsciously speak in such a manner that strong adjectives agree with strong nouns, weak adjectives with weak nouns. Not knowing the meaning of declension, they neverthless use the adjectives, nouns and personal pronouns in the required case. They never make the mistake of having a weak noun as the object of a strong verb. They never miss putting the object of either strong or weak verb in the accusative case, nor putting the noun in the dative case after a preposition. They never use the plural instead of the dual number or vice versa.

I do not claim that our language is perfect, but we believe that it is as grammatical in its expression as any other and we also believe that all the other Algonkian dialects are about the same as ours.

It is written somewhere that a vocabulary of Indian names so beautiful and expressive would be not only curious but valuable, and if someone could explain the meaning of them in an intelligible manner, his work would be much appreciated. This indeed is a difficult task, because the Indian names often have two or three consonants together in their make-up, and because the Indians generally speak in a low tone of voice it is hard to catch the mixed sound of several consonants together. For this reason we may suppose that in many case the pronunciation was not fully understood by those unacquainted with the language and the names were written accordingly.

The names are generally composed of a radical, a prefix or suffix or both as Massa Jos Ek.

Prefix Massa means big; Jos - Mountain - Ek is the dative case of Jos meaning to. Jos itself means small mountain. Massa jos ek would then mean - To the great of small mountains or Massachusetts.

We can fairly assume that the Abenaki language was spoken long before the discovery of America and relying upon the valuable records left us by the venerable first Missionaries to the Indians we can affirm that it has not changed much since then. It is a primitive language since it is not at all like the European languages, and if we offer our grammar, it is chiefly to show our White brothers what kind of language is ours.

Henry Lorne Masta,
St-Francis Indian Reserve,
Odanak, P. Q.

PART I

ABENAKI INDIAN LEGENDS AND STORIES

MAGUAK TA WOBANAKIAK

Niga agua n8wat Maguak waiji kadonal8nozsa W8banakia taagata achi kdagihi aln8ba wadagui 8nkaw8bagzijik wess8gnaikok, Waijiwi wbemi nb8n8zsa siboikok ta nbessikok pami kiminkadit ta8lawiba pmadialidida ni 8zhagiwi nami8dida W8banakia ala yugik wichow8 nitta wgimina-l8n8 wz8miga 8ndaba wawjeskawiwi wgizi saka-w8wiw8 ayag8batta agm8w8 n8wi paamalo-didda.

Ni 8zoka yugik W8banakiak wdaladialin8zsa mad8balodni-tekwok ni Maguak wawaldamodit ali n8nabiwi nigik chowi naosadit niadoji skow8l8dit adali wli kwz8wa8mak, nospakaak ta wl8bame-guak nopaiwi laguiwi almi agwdai. Enni 8nka W8banakiak attali ntami 8tsidit naihl8diji. Pajilhl8dit nawa nidali nitta wn8dagahl8n8 sibiwi pabachitodit mziwi kawi kagnaba awanihi wdali wesko-k8gon8. Askwa ni ali aidit wawdagu8mek ni adoji kokokhas kdok-wazit yuta t8m8 pasodawiwi nitta mina kdak adoji kdokwazit t8m8 nopaiwi ni adoji pasgo kchai idak 8nda nigik kokokhassak kadokwazijik, Maguak ka nigik, askawana kwilawa8nach ta migak-k8m8nch nitta wski alnobak wdidamn8 kaalatta migak8m8nach ni m8manni wm8joldin8 Kwilaw8bam8dit kokokhassa spemek abazikok, nitta n8gaiwi kchai wnamion pasgowa, 8lawiki pita wli k8dəbozsa wanaskwakwa kchi abazik ni wdihl8n kia Magua Kz8dal-damana km8wzow8gan nitta pn8dawa ni kaala wben8dawan ni kanwa wiwhibabil8n sibiwi attahl8mek pazgo san8ba waji nana-w8bam8t, ni kdagik wdalmosan8 awassiwi kwilaw8bam8dit kdagihi kokokhassa, 8nda kwina n8wasawiak ni kizi wmeskaw8n8 ta n8bi wdeli li8n8 ta8lawita'na kdak, ni askwa wdalmossan8 awassiwi ni kanwa sazalakiwi adoji idak'na kchai ni kizi Maguak wz8khosan8 ni kdachowi migakanana t8nitta p8bay8moik ni mziwi kdagik wida-men8. 8h88, oh8o, chowi kaalata kaalata! Nigatta n8gaiwessi nigizi W8banakiak wwolwan8 ni sibiwi kjawai polwadit nitta Maguak wnosokozin8 t8nibanawa niga adoji awdimek ta awdimek li mziwi matta8mek maguak wibiwitta 8da ntamia kokokhas nagaki kajita-waguaz8 ni mil8n mijw8gan alham8d li payoda wajiaawid. Ni aska-mad ni aliwit8zik kokokhas (Coocoocache).

————

THE IROQUOIS AND ABENAKIS

It is said that the Iroquois Indians used to be the enemies of the Abenakis and of all the other Indians of the Algonquin stock and did their utmost to exterminate them. They always had lurking places along the rivers and around small lakes and acted as when hunting wild beasts. They lay in wait to kill them. They never faced the Abenakis defiantly for unless they were by far the more numerous they never got the best of them.

It is further related that when the Abenakis were hunting at a certain place on the St-Maurice River, and the Iroquois knowing approximately the time when the hunters would come down the river, a number of them went up to a point of land from where they could see quite a distance higher up the river. The Abenakis on their way home usually spent half a day and sometimes stopped over night at this beautiful place. On this occasion, as soon as they had landed they began to examine the place to see if there were any footprints, but instantly they heard the hooting or cry of an owl (kokokhas) not far distant. In a few minutes they heard another owl further away. Then an old man said, "These are not the hootings of owls but of Iroquois. Be that as it may, let them be searched out and opposed," and the young men said, "Yes, yes, let us look for them and drive them away." And they all went very cautiously looking here and there on the ground and in the trees, finally the old man saw one of the owls in the shape of an Iroquois whose hiding place was deftly planned and made on the top of a tall tree. He called him saying, "Iroquois, if you estimate your life worth living come right down." As soon as he touched the ground he was securely tied hands and feet and left in the care of one man; the others went on further and soon discovered the other owl Iroquois. The two prisoners were treated in like manner. The rest of the party kept following the trail until suddenly the old man stopped and said, "Our enemies are now coming on and are near at hand. We are not women, we can and must fight to the bitter end notwithstanding the cost", and all said, "Yes, yes!"

The Iroquois were approaching not knowing that their game was so near, but the old man acted and spoke in a manner to make them beleive that the Abenakis were afraid and at the same time he feigned as if he and his men were running away. The Iroquois hearing and seeing what was going on could not overcome the temptation to capture their prey, but unfortunately the old man suddenly turned round and began to fight followed by his men doing the same, and they easily won the battle having killed everyone of their enemies except the owl first captured who was sent home minus his ears, but loaded with provisions.

Ever since this memorable event the place has been called Kokokhas (Coocoocache).

II

NISWACK WSKIAIN8BAK NIKES TA NOJMIGAN8T CHAJIG8WI WL8MAHODWAK

Nik:—N'Odossa Kaozenitekw-ok.

Noj:—8da Kodossawen.

Nik:—8zokokita n'odassan.

Noj:—8datagna koji wdossawen.

Nik:—T8niba koji kiziidamen ali 8nda wdossawa.

Noj:—Wz8miga 8nda t8m8 aiwi wskidkamikwa kaozen'itekw, kagui-
bani amojka idamoo kaozen'itekw? 8nda kiona al8ndwaakw
kwaj8nmownana ni klozw8gan "Kaozen" 8nda kawi idom-
winnokw.

Nik:—Kanwa awanochak wdli witamen8 "La Rivière aux vaches."

Noj:—Ni nawaaba Aln8baiwi chowi livit8z8 Kaoz'itekw ondaki
Kaozen'itekw; kanwa 8nda achi t8m8 aiwi yo Kaoz'itekw.

Nik:—Kagui nawaba kia kdliwitamen?

Noj:—Ndeliwitamenga kawassen'itekw wji aalest8zik ali n8wat to-
dossaikza nitali pdewgl8msen massali wagalokaik, abaziak
poskwihlak, kadajabkahlak ta kawihlak enni aliwit8zik kawassen, ni achi waji liwitozik ni sibo kawassen'itekw.

TWO YOUNG MEN, NIKES AND NOJMIGAN8T (*WEAK KNEE*) DISCUSSING.

Nik:—I have been to Kaozen'itekwok.

Noj:—You have not been there.

Nik:—I am sure that I have been there.

Noj:—You have never been there.

Nik:—How can yeu say that I never was there.

Noj:—Because there is no Kaozen'itkekw in the world. What could
be the meaning of Kaozen? There is no such a meaningless
word in our language.

Nik:—But the French people call it La Rivière aux vaches.

Noj:—In that case it should be Kaoz'itekw in Indian and not
Kao-en'itekw but there is no Kaozitekw here anyway.

Nik:—What then do you call it?

Noj:—I call it Kawassen'itekw because according to tradition a whirlwind once caused havoc along that stream breaking and uprooting trees. The tumbling of trees is called Kawassen hence the river itself is called Kawassen'itekw.

The compound noun Kawassen'itekw is declined:—
Nom:—Kawassen'itekw
Gen:—Kawassen'itekw'i
Dat:—Kawassen'itekwok
Acc:—Kawassen'itekw
Abl:—Kawassen'itekwok

III

PIAL TA AZ8

Pial:—Nid8ba Az8 pasguen ta 8toji wlidbin8gwzian t8ni nawa kd8ll8wzin?

Az8:—Sawigatta ni 8toji wlalmegwwa.

Pial:—Kam8ji nowat kdakwi namihollen; t8m8 kwodkanni?

Az8:—8h88 niga anegi waji pay8a Maine.

Pial:—Niga nid8ba kia nawa atoba kizi hlin idamoik Kennebec River?

Az8:—Chowi, idamoo gani kinnebak sibo.

Pial:—Nia kanwa ndelsedam ali kmahom-nogak W8banakiak liwilh-l8mgeza achi Kennebessinnoak ali waijiwi sibowikok ta nbessikok pmi aidiza ni agua almidbihl8k li taakwi wilh8-n8zsa agm8w8 ta wzibomw8 Kinnebak.

Az8:—Nid8ba 8nda kmaw8ztawi ta 8nda achi nia kmawoztolo, Idozijga niziwitta kol8mmabna.

PIAL AND AZ8

Peter:—My friend John! You are looking as well as ever. How are you?

John:—I am feeling quite well, thank you.

Peter:—I have not seen you for a long time, have you been away?

John:—Yes, I have just come from Maine.

Peter:—Well then my friend you can perhaps tell me the meaning of Kennebec River.

John:—Certainly. It means a river full or nearly full up to its banks.

Peter:—But I have heard that our great grandfathers were also called Kanibassinoak because they lived near big rivers and lakes and this designation of themselves and of their river was afterwards changed into Kanibak.

John:—My friend you are not pleased with my explanation nor am I with yours, but let us say that we both are right.

IV

WAWAN8GIT TA M8LADAKW

Wana:—Nid8ba M8ladakw kia nat8wi milgakanian alakssa ato koli oji wawiton Koatekwok.

Mol:—Koatekwok ennigani 8nka Awanochak ali witamodit Coaticook. Nialo kala n'oli wawaldamen: Oji chig8wteguagani Vermont ni talli s8gdahla kzibonnokw, Ailsig8tekwok. Koatekw'ni kinni p8ntekwoo pab8miwi mail oji odanak n8bi aliwiswik ni waji m8ja p8ntekwwik.

Wana:—Kawinawa ni waji liwit8zik Koatekw?

Mol:—Wz8migaato pita msalozhanik nitali koaak taagata achi askwa wdain8.

WAWAN8GIT AND M8LADAKW

Wana:—My friend M8ladakw as you are habitually travelling here and there you are perhaps well acquainted with Koatekwok?

Mol:—Koatekwok is the river which is called Coaticook by the Whites. I indeed know it well. It has its source in Vermont and falls into our river Alsigontekwok (St-Francis River). There are many rapids and falls in its course beginning at about one mile from the City of the same name.

Wawa:—But why was it called Koatekwok?

Mol:—Because there must have been a large quantity of pine trees there and there are some even now.

Koa means pine, suffix tekw means river. Koatekw means pine river.

Declined.

Nom:—Koatekw—*The Pine River.*
Gen:—Koatekw'i—*Of The Pine River.*
Dat:—Koatekwok—*To The Pine River.*
Acc:—Koatekw—*The Pine River.*
Abl:—Koatekwok—*From The Pine River.*

V

NATANIS TA SABADIS

Nat:—Nid8ba Sabadis kiziba kia witamawin kaguessi sibo ni aliwit8zik Connecticut ta t8ndaka pamtekwak?

Sab:—Niba k8kizilla 8nda kwawaldamowen Kwnitekw ta t8ndaka pamtekwak!

Nat:—Ondaki n'wawaldamowen wz8miga 8nda kwina yo nia nmessali pmiaiwen.

Sab:—T8ni nawa kia wajiawian?

Nat:—Yoga 8lawi wajiawia ni kanwa 8nda kwina yo lakwkwamigiwi ndihaiwen.

Sab:—T8ninawa kwina massali aiyan.

Nat:—Adaliga msali aiya (Australia). Chaga nikw8bi witamawi'ni nadodmolan liwlaldamana.

Sab:—Ni ato kaala ndeliwlaldamen ta wig8damiwi k'wawaldamenga kiona al8dwaakw klozwogan li m8jataga nspiwi kwna, kwne, kwni, kwno, kwn8, idamoo ali ni kawi wit8zik kwnak; k8dak

kwna kwam idamoo kwanak abazi.

kwne gisgad idamoo kwanak kizokw,

kwni tbakad idamoo kwanak tebokw,

kwn8 bagak idamoo kwanak al8bagak,

kwni tekw idamoo kwanak tekw ala sibo.

Ni 8zoka w8bigigik kadawi idamodit Kwnitekwok idamok "Connecticut" kanwaga Aln8ba agmatta paami 8nimgwezo wji ni ondaki awani kdak wz8mi 8nda tabi mhz8dwawi ta 8nda tabi mkedonawiwi wajiba kisi pabaki witak klozw8genal.

Nat:—Kaalanawani Kwnitekw kwnitegua?

Sab:—Chowi 8ndagabani liwit8ziwi chaga 8nda kweniteguawi.

Nat:—T8ninawa kwena ta t8ni pamijoassek.

Sab:—Oji m8ja chig8wtegua New Hampshire ta Canada ni todtegua nansawiwi New Hampshire ta Vermont ni oji wbikag8kamen Massachusetts ta Connecticut ni n8ji tali s8gdahla Long-Island Sound. Pab8mwi yawategua kasta mail kwena.

NATANIS AND SABADIS

Nat:—My friend Sabadis can you tell me which is the river called Connecticut and its course?

Sab:—Is it possible that you do not know Kwenitekw and its course!

Nat:—It is true, it is because I have never lived around here very much.

Sab:—Where then do you keep yourself?

Nat:—I live mostly in Australia; now tell me if you please what I have asked you.

Sab:—Yes, and very willingly too. You know that in our language a word beginning with the prefix Kwena, Kweni, Kweno or Kwen8 it means long and the suffix tells what is long.

The suffix "tekw" means *river*

Kwenitekw means *long river*.

Kwena plus Kwam means *long stick*.

Kwene plus gisgad means *long day*.

Kweni plus tbakad means *long night*.

But the English instead of saying Kweni-tekw-ok say Connecticut. However, the Indian is more to blame for this than anyone else, because he speaks too low and does not open his mouth wide enough so as to articulate his words properly.

Nat:—Well is Kwenitekw really a long river?

Sab:—Assuredly. It would not be so called if it were not so.

Nat:—Where, then, is its source, course and mouth?

Sab:—Its source is in New Hampshire; its course between New Hampshire and Vermont and across Massachusetts and Connecticut and empties into Long Island Sound. It is about 400 miles long.

Kweni-tekw declined.

Nom:—Kwenitekw—*Connecticut.*
Gen:—Kwenitekw'i—*Of Connecticut.*
Dat:—Kwenitekwok—*To Connecticut.*
Acc:—Kwenitekw—*Connecticut.*
Tbl:—Kwenitekw ok—*From connecticut.*

VI

ALMONSKA TA WESWAKWIG8T

Al:—Nsassis Weswakwig8t kisi kia knahnodamen al8kwkwihl8t kwetguettiahl8t ta kawessani waji liwilhl8mgeza?

Wes:—8h88 wakassokamikwzoak ka agua W8banakiak wdainn8zsa Atman'i sibok Wdalokaw8ganw8 wawhawi lignozsa waji 8gmikamek ta namaskamek.

Plasao Simo saz8gli wski aln8ba pita 8lawi nt8wtemassa ni kanwa wbamaldamen wnamaskan 8daki t8nitta kdak kawi wdellalokanni nawa wigaw8jiwi wdabazimal ta wellogosmal pakwsada, ni wmit8gwzsa adoji hlegot aliji kaguessa li sakp8 pajitbihl8t illi namaskadep chaga wdalmi paguazikadamen wdalokaw8gan. Ni kaala salakiwi wzakp8ztamen kawi ali tikkakwasik al8miwi ala naguiwi wdolek nitta achi wdalmi ladah8bin ali pita sakp8 wagawbagosaik sibo ni wdoji kispahl8n ta wdoji sagzin waji kwaguaji n8dagahl8t akw8bi nabiwi.

Kchai pita wn8nabi wawolgo wnam8na ali pilwidah8t ta ali pilwalokat ni wdihl8n: "N'nam8n kam8ji nwig8dam namiholan 8ttoji nikw8bi wlidbahokaan." Ni wskinos wdidamen. "8ndaga ni mozhagida8mgwadwi wz8miga n'kizi kwetguettiahl8 ta alwa n'baskejba." Ni enna Plasoa askamat ali 8ji wizit kweguettiahl8t.

Al:—Nsassis kawi nawa waji kia liwilgahan weswakwig8t?

Wes:—Wz8miga ndawanochwi lawka. Kadawi nawa wawaldamana achi kaguessa kia waji liwilgahan Alm8ska niga kdilhen:

"Koji gani liwilgan ali kzis-gol p8paami piwsessek ta ali 8nda kwina kawi wawaldamowan aik wskidkamlkwa.

ALMONSKA AND WESWAKWIG8T

Al:—Uncle Weswakwig8t have you ever heard the story of Kwet-guettiahl8t and why he was so called?

Wes:—Yes, There were a few families of Abenakis settled at (Atman'i sibok) Etchemin River. Their occupation was making snow shoes and fishing. Plasowa Simo a sturdy young man was very skilful at framing and lacing fancy snow shoes, but he preferred fishing to anything else, and many a time his frame-sticks and gut strings would get dry while he was fishing.

One day his father told him that if he continued to neglect his work something terrible might happen to him. The boy took no head of the warning but the thing did happen shortly after, when he was fishing. All at once he heard a frightful roaring noise in or under his conoe and it seemed to him that there was a great disturbance of the water in the river. He was so surprised and so scared that he immediately made for the shore. The old man soon noted that his son had changed his ways for he went fishing no more but was steadily making snow shoes. One day his father told him. "My son. I am glad to see you doing so well now." The boy said, "No wonder, my canoe capsized and I came darn near getting drowned."

Al:—Uncle please tell me the reason why you are called Weswakwig8t?

Wes:—It is because there is some resemblance between a white man and me. Let me tell you also why you are called Alm8nska. It is because your eyes are so darn small and because you know so little of what is going on in the world.

Etchemin from Atman.

Atman means *gut strlng* used in the middle part of snow shoes.

Alm8nska means *mole.*

Weswakwig8t means *hairy leg.*

Kwetguettiahl8t means *he whose canoe capsized.*

Atman or Etchemin falls into the St-Lawrence a few miles above Levis, Que.

It is a fact that a roaring sound at Atman or Etchemin is sometimes heard even at Quebec.

VII

SQUANDO TA SAMBO

Squan:—Nid8ba Sambo Kwawaldamen kia t8nio ni Mickinack River ta kaguessa ni waji liwit8zik?

Sam:—W8banakigani wdainap ligadinwaiwi ta wdoji wli wawaldamenap ni sibo ta8lawitta wigw8m t8nba wdagwdalhl8n nangem8jiwi, wl8gwiwi n8bitta ta8lawi kisgadiwi waijiwi nan8wtegua tojihla, ni pasguida wnahilon anegita nakihl8t kizos ni salakiwitta adoji t8m8 wskijipodaazik wdol nitta adoji kwaguataak ni kawi awakad wdemhiganis lit8guat ta8lawitta ba tagad8ziga sen ni wdoji 8zhagidahozin waji 8nda kizi kawikw ni angitta s8gh8bak wn8ji pabachiton ni adali 8zhag8wzi dep kanwa 8nda kawi wdeli pilwinamowen ni kanwa mina achakwiwik wmeskaw8n kta 8dowi kchi tolba wmiknakwoma toji msegilo waji mziwitta nak8iwi kizi tali wlibdi k8ttlezit. Ni askamat ni aliwit8zik Miknakw'i sibo. Tali ni s8gdahla Madobalodn'itekwok pabomiwi n8nninska kasta mail oji Mad8balodnik.

SQUANDO AND SAMBO

Squan:—My friend Sambo can you tell me which is Mickinack River and why it is so called?

Sam:—Yes. There was an Abenaki who lived there, a few years, and knew that river as well as his wigwam. Why he used to go up and down the river at all times of the day and night and never met with any obstacle, but one evening soon after sunset as he went down his canoe slipped on something hard which he struck with his hatchet and the sound of the blow was as if a stone was hit; he was so surprised and amazed that he could not sleep that night. At dawn he went back to look for the mysterious thing which puzzled him and found no change whatever in the place and was all the more astonished, but the next morning he discovered a very large turtle whose shell was so big that it did safely and entirely hide itself in it, hence the name Miknakw'i Sibo, the Turtle River. It falls into the St-Maurice about 50 miles from the St-Lawrence.

Declined.

Nom:—Miknakw.
Gen:—Miknakw'i.
Dat:—Miknakwok.
Acc:—Miknakw.
Abl:—Miknakwok.

VIII

CHIMI TA SOZI

Chim:—Nad8gues Sozi kia nat8wi milgi wawizian kwawaldamen ni kawi idamoo "Magermette?"

Sozi:—Kia nawa 8nda kwawtamowen?

Chim:—8ndakl.

Sozi:—Nibat8ni idam8na Majalmit?

Chim:—8! Nigaki nwawtamen ta8lawiba pawanalit.

Sozi:—8h88 kma8wi wawtamen ni kanwa awanochak wdelawakan8 ni Margermette ta8lawi wizwogan wji wajo, sibo ta wnigan.

Chim:—T8ninawa 'ni oji pajidbihla?

Sozi:—Niga kdilhem. Kmaomnogakka W8banakiak ojiaozhanik kenebakwog Maine Waj8nazhanik patlih8za kagakimgodiji. Ni salakiwi wdilgon8 ali chowi ngalgodit wji ali sogm8i patlih8z pedgi wikwim8t lli N'kebak. Nitta achakwiwik podawazwinoak wdeligiston8 waji wakaswak aln8bak losadit N'kebak waji wli wawtamakh8dit s8gm8i patlih8za adguikwi chowalm8dit wpatlih8zmow8. Ni kaala wdelosann8zsa ta wli nton8shanik wz8mi enna ma8wi patlih8z ta kdak plajm8n kassiwi nigik W8banakiak ta pasgo Atman'i alnoba w'oji m8jin8 N'kbak li kenebakwog. Ni wa m8mjeslawilhl8mek enna kakinos alwaza ta enna achi tabinaw8za ta pamhol8za w8bigiliji ni wdagwdalh8n8zsa Atman'i sibo ta mziwikawi w8wlosaozsa li pay8dit manosai sibok enniba achewi nailhlodidep waji ntokamodit ta agwdahl8dit kokwi ta molsem'i siboal ta achi Magermette ni kanwa w8wahla

wnailh8n8zsa Doaguam, Wallastekw ta Saz8'i siboal li m8la-
m8lami Madawaska.

Ni nidali sibiwi Atman'i aln8ba pakaldak, taaki askwa
chadzo wgaam8mlomen ali wanihl8t. Pajoldidid ni mziwi
attassi pasgo mam8dan adoji sawsanit 8lawiki naihlak niji
wlamiz nikw8bi wji ali chowi agwdahl8dit pedgidida ni
kanwa 8nda amojka pela 8dabiwiak nitta wm8ja agwda-
sinn8 msik8jid8ni ni kanwa pita nabiwi ni kizi wm8ja no-
damm8n8 mijw8gan nitta achi mliksanw8gan ni lli mina
pay8dit manosa'i sibok ni kizi wmanosan8. Niga 8nka ni
waji liwit8zik Manosa'i sibo. Kanwa chowilwak waji kwaguaji kizi s8pkannidit. Nigaki wzig8wzowi pay8n8 adali
s8gdahl8k Magermette. Ni wdali chanabin8ni, kisidah8zi-
dit wz8lalitamen8 t8nitta kawi. Ni enna Atmani al8ba adoji
m8ja 8nim8t wpatlih8zma idak "owagani kchi majigwinowi
patlih8z; kchi maji mdawleno wji ali nia akwalmit, ali
kadonalit; ali pawanalit ta majalmit, enni wadtak kd8pchi
mziwi kskwal8moldinana" askwa ni ali majiklozit ni pat-
t8guat ali pazgo W8banaki kizi nhl8t moza nitta adoji mina
idak" niga nikw8bi wli pakalmeguat ali idama allak, wz8mi
knamiton8 ta mziwi kwawaldamnana ali angitta owa mdawleno 8nadah8zit nitta knabajilinana. Kanwa wzaakaw8ganw8
asma matanasktawi sakp8 kzitan wji ali yutta wajok ojijoak
ayag8 mzewi wmelkassanw8ganw8 ta wnitatw8ganw8 awa-
kadit waji s8bosadit ni achi nita saakashanik waji wniga-
dit li awassadena.

Chim:—Nadogues Sozi wliwnini adoji wli kagakimian. Nikw8bi
nwawtamen Kaguessa waji pasguenwik wisw8gan Magermette wji wajo, sibo ta wnigan-wzomiga enni tali nigik
kedm8gi aln8bak ta pamkannikh8diji adali manosadit ta
adali alwa kwskwi majalmegodit, kanwa 8nda ngiz8ji ni
damen ali kaala Atmani aln8ba pawanal8mgeza. Nadogues
niba mjessala li wlidaa8na kwittamawin idamowik aliwiswik attassi sibo adodkanidiza nigig aln8bak nspiwi wpatlih-
8zmow8.

Sozi:—Alwaga ato mziwi kwawaldamnal.

1—Etchemin Atman'i sibo Atman skahla'i pikon awakamek
waji temamek 8gmak. Niga kwina nitojiwi adali8mgep
8gmak.

2—Famine river Manosa'i sibo Niga adali m8ja manosaa-
didep aln8bak.

3—Chaudiere Kokw'i sibo toji kzitan waji mamsegilodit kokwak.

4—Riviere du Loup Molsem'i sibo wji ali msalodiza Molsemok.

5—Magermette Majalmit wji ali Atman'i aln8ba li wl8mawaldagza ali pawanalegot patlih8za.

6—Doaquam Ktaquam'i sibo wji ali ktaquamikag.

7—St-John Saz8.

8—Madawaska Madobaskika.

9—Kenebec Kinebak wji ali psanbak ala alwa psanbak.

10—Wallastekw wji ali wallaskidmak.

Chim:—Nadogues Sozi niba askwa pasguen kawi kwigi nadodmolen kaguessani aln8bak aliwitamodiza N'kebak ta kaguessa ni wji.

Sozi:—Kchi odanagani aln8bak ali witamodidep. N'kebak ta agwa ni wji liwit8zosa ali wigaw8jiwi nkebak pami tapsakaak. Ni awanochak agm8w8 wdeli witamen8 Quebec wji ali saagi idamodid N'kebak.

CHIMI AND SOZI

Chim:—Cousin Sozi, you who have a general knowledge of things can you tell me the meaning of Magermette?

Sozi:—Why! don't you understand that?

Chim:—No, I do not.

Sozi:—Would you understand it if I said Majalmit?

Chim:—O! I do understand that. It means he bewitched me.

Sozi:—You are right but the French use Magermette as a proper name of a Mountain, River and carry or portage.

Chim:—How did it all happen?

Sozi:—Well, I'll tell you. Our great grandfathers, the Abenakis were originally from Maine, on Kenebec River. They had a priest to teach them, who one day told them that he was to leave being recalled to Quebec, by His Lordship the Bishop. The next day the Council decided to send a delegation to Quebec to convince the Bishop of their sincere attachment to their priest and of their great need of him and their great desire to have him back. Their request was complied with. The same priest and another Frenchman the Abenaki Indians and one Etchemin Indian left Quebec for the Kenebec Mission. The last named Indian was the guide or leader and the guardian of the Frenchmen, they being in his canoe. They went via the Etchemin river and everything went all right until they reached the source of a river which was afterwards named "Famine". They should have gone down this river to meet the Chaudiere river; the Riviere du Loup and the Magermette, instead they went down the Doaquam, the Wallastekw and St-John until they reached the Madawaska. It was there and then only that the leader was convinced of his mistake and reluctantly admitted it. Though they went down the stream yet they were all tired out and everyone uttered a mournful sound when they got there. But without taking any rest they went up pulling very hard to make up time; unfortunately their strength and provisions were fast getting exhausted and they were starving when they again reached Famine river. Hence the name Famine river. Yet they were bound to go through and they reached Magermette river, but they were very miserable. Unable to go any farther they stopped there fully resigned to their fate.

The leader then began to blame his priest saying, "It is through the wickedness of this sorcerer that we are now starving", and while he was yet accusing the priest some one brought word that one of the Abenakis had killed a moose. The leader got up and said, "You have now the proof that what I say is true because we all know that the moment the sorcerer relents then are we immediately relieved." But their hardship was not yet over, the current, owing to the proximity of the mountain, was so strong that it required all their strength and ability to get through and they also had much trouble to carry over the mountain.

Chim:—Cousin Sozi, I thank you for the information you have given me. I now understand how it is that only one name "Magermette" is given to a mountain, river and carry.

It was at these several places that the poor Indians and those in their charge most suffered from hunger and hardship but I am not ready to say that the Atman Indian was really bewitched.

Dear Cousin, if you would be so kind as to tell me the meaning of the name of each river that these Indians came to, I would be very thankful.

Sozi:—I think you know all the names.

1—Etchemin, Atman means *gut string* used in lacing snow-shoes. Etchemin river, Atman'i sibo was the chief snow-shoe manufacturing place.

2—Famine river, Manosa'i sibo is where these Indians were starving, hence the name.

3—Chaudiere river, Kokwi sibo means *whirl-pool* river. Kokw means *kettle or boiler,* hence the French call the river Chaudiere.

4—Riviere du loup, Molsem'i sibo means *Wolf river.*

5—Magermette, Majalmit means *he bewitched me.* The Atman Indian beleived that his priest bewitched him.

6—Doaquam river, Ktaquam'i sibo means *a river of a thick forest of big trees.*

7—St-John, Saz8.

8—Kenebec, Kinebak means *full or nearly full.*

9—Madawaska, Mad8baskika means *grass to the water's edge.*

10—Wallastekw means *shallow river.*

Chim:—Dear cousin, please allow me one more question. What is the meaning of N'Kebak and why did the Indians call it so?

Sozi:—N'Kebak is the name of a city and the Indians called it so, because a certain portion of the lower part of it was often inundated and remained under water for sometime. The French call it Quebec because it is hard for them to say N'Kebak.

IX

W8BANAKIAK TALI SWONTON VT.

Wji akw8bi id8zik ta akw8bi awikh8zik, angitta W8bigijik m8ja aidit Swanton Vt. pab8miwi 1790 akw8bigadek, wdain8zsa'ni nonninska kassokamigzoak W8banakiak wajiawijik Alsig8ntekwok ta msaltozhanik skamonkik8nal ni kanwa waji kizi wl8wzidid ayag8 achi namaskaadid ta nadialidid ta sawi ayag8 nopassadid. Ni k8-

dak pasgueda wakaswak wdali weskok8gon8zsa Magua, kwahliwi
Sal8nnaki Nbesek. Maguak paamalozhanik 8ndaki agm8w8 taaba
wmataoogw8bani chaga 8nda wguitaalmegwown8 kanwa achi agm8-
w8 wzakp8wlegw8 nitta tali wibiwi wdasko-8ldin8 ta8lawiba niswak
pezoak 8mpchi kadawi awdidida. Ni W8banakiak kadopidid azi
pazgo wmow8n manhakw8gana ni sibiwi kistodid waji migakadit
nitta achi adoji m8ja nawadwadid, pmeg8did ta kwakwah8midid ni
kadonalgodijikizi polwaadid, wmamhlawi kog8l wan8 maguwak ni
onka waji askwa liwilh8mek Magwak. Ni 8zidaiwi agm8w8 wdeli-
wihl8n8 W8banàkia "Adirondacks" manhakw8gana mowojik.

ABENAKI INDIANS AT SWANTON VT.

According to tradition and to some record when the Whites
first settled at Swanton, Vt., in 1790, approximately, the St-Francis
Abenaki Indians had there about fifty wigwams with large corn
fields, but in order to make a fine living they needed some fish and
meat; therefore they had to go fishing and hunting and sometimes
did go quite far. For instance a few of them were one day inter-
cepted by a greater number of Iroquois near Saranac Lake and all
would undoubtedly have been killed but for the great fear that the
one and the other party had of each other. They both simply remained on their guard even as two wild cats do when about to fight.
Finally the Abenakis being very hungry began, one at a time, to eat
the pith of a pine tree, after which they decided to fight and at once
started on a wardance shouting and yelling. The Iroquois slyly
withdrew and when the Abenakis perceived that their enemies were
leaving they cried out aloud "Magowak, Magowak" "Cowards, Cowards," and that is the reason why the Iroquois are still called Maguak. In return they called the Abenakis "Adirondacks"—bark eaters.

X

LOL8 TA SAKSO

Lol8:—N'ndadanis Sakso k'kiziba kia hlin awanina mdawleno?
Sakso:—Kwinata kzaagi nadodmawi Lol8, kanwa kdilhenga, nia
    alidah8zia. Mdawlenogana t8na ali kwaguialzit, wh8ga ta
    mjejako li madah8ndok waji llalokad t8ni alchow-aldam8-
    god ni 8zidaiwi wmilgon mliksanw8gan waji kizi 8zhagi
    wawizwinoid ta waji kizi 8zhagalokad. Ni k8dak agua
    pazgueda Maguak yo Alsig8ntekwok ali n8zkozidid ni ma8-

wi wibiwitta wdain8zsa kchaiak, phanemok ta aw8zsizak,
t8ninawaba nigatta alwa mziwi matta8n8. Ni kanwa achakwiwik san8bak pedgi pay8did nitta wbodawazin8 mdawleno idak niji allalokadid. Ni mdawleno kizi azinakwa-
blem8d wdidamen n'namiy8k kadonalgowaguik pmi wanih-
lak, manozsak ta kizi nawji kwskwal8mwak. 8nda kizi
m8wossowiak. N'nami8 pab8miwi yawinska aijik mnaanizek, kizi nabajilwak ta mliki mitsoldowak. 8ndoba ni nitta
oji m8joldiwn8. Niga nitta kn8zkaw8nana, 8ndaba kiona
knihl8pena kchaiak, phanemok ta aw8zsizak kanwaji yogik
8nda amoohka pazgo oji polwawen. Nigaki nigik pami wa-
nihl8jik kizi mziwi machinak. Wdali pay8n8ni wl8gwiwi
tadbog8 mnaanizek aoldidid Maguak. Ni agua nizwak W8ba-
makiak: Tmakwa ta Moskwas wbikag8 kamguinn8 ni snojiwi mnaanizek wz8kwassinn8, ma8wi 8mpchi mitsoldowak
Maguak, Ni s8gm8 adoji idak "T'cha nguilotah8n Wobanaki."
ni adoji mamhlawakad kchi wskan li snojiwi. Nigaki na
wawlitah8n Moskwassa wdepek. Nitta Tmakwa wgedoban8n
wid8ba waji 8nda waolwakw. Ni kizi mziwi Maguak kaol-
didid ni agma adoji tedozek mziwi wiguaolal ni sibiwl
pedgi kamguid li wid8baikok. Nitta mziwi W8banakiak
wgiz8joldin8 ni kanwa m8manni wbikag8n8 nanni achakwak. Ni kizi wli wiwnikaw8did Magua nitta wm8ja miga-
k8m8n8 sibiwi mamhlawi kwakwah8midid ta mziwi wmat-
ta8w8. Ni oji wnimakwhamn8 mziwi Magua'8depal kw-
nakwam'ikok ni ulil wiwnig8badon8 mnaanizek. Ni 8nka
enni mnaanis waji liwit8zik "Wdepsek." Ni nikwobi knadod-
mollen Lol8 t8ni wa mdawleno wd8lli kizi lli pazobin ta
lli nodamen llategua kasta mail chaga 8nda wdaguiwi ma-
dah8ndwi alokaw8ganek?

LOL8 AND SAKSO

Lol8:—Uncle Sakso can you tell me what is a wizard?

Sakso:—Your question is quite difficult for me to answer but I'll
give you my opinion. A wizard is a person who has given
up himself body and soul to the devil to do his (devil's)
will, and in return receives from him a certain power ena-
bling him to know and do wonderful things.

For instance the Iroquois once came down to the St-
Francis River to fall upon the Abenakis just at a time when
there were present only old men, women and children, and

these were nearly all killed in a short time. But on the next day when men came back they at once held a council as to what they should do. It was decided to submit their case to a wizard and to do whatever he would say. The wizard after many abjurations in his tiny bark tent came out and said:"I see our secret enemies. They have lost their way and are suffering and dying of hunger. They cannot stick together and those who went astry are all dead. I see another group about forty in number who seem to be more fortunate then the others. They are on a small island and are enjoying eating the flesh of an animal they have just killed. But their fate is no better than that of the others because we are going for them right away. We will not kill old men, women and children. but I declare that not one of these on the Island will escape."

It was night when they reached the place opposite the Island temporarily occupied by the Iroquois. Two Abenakis, Tmakwa (Beaver) and Moskwas (Muskrat) dived to the Island and there just their heads were out of water. The Iroquois were eating and the Chief said "Tcha I am going to hit an Abenaki with this" and he threw aimlessly but with all his might a big bone hitting Moskwas on the head and Tmakwa to prevent an alarm immediately held his friend under water. When the Iroquois were all asleep he cut open all their canoes and then dived back to his friends. The Abenakis got ready at once but they slowly got over at dawn and as soon as they had closely surrounded them they began the slaughter, yelling loudly and every one of the Iroquois group was killed and the head of each one of them was stuck at the end of a pole and all the poles planted around the Island, and that is the reason why that Island was called "Wdepsek" Head's Island.

And now, Lol8, I ask you how was it possible to the wizard to see and hear hundreds of miles away if not through the power and subtlety of the devil.

Lol8:—Uncle, I believe all what you say.

XI

NAGAKO TA MOZIS

Mag:—Nzassis kowawalm8ssa'na kia t8m8 tojiwi, Aln8ba aliwizid Chila ala Kw8gwnas?

Moz:—8h88, nleguas, Wess8gnagani aliwihl8mek oji ali chilaid ta kw8gwnaskid. Wnibawin8bani yudali, ntami S8gm8, Llobal wdoza aliwizid Soli8n. Enna n8kshwa lli wawalmegwzop ali pita wligid, wlidbin8gwzid ta waw8dak Wgezaldamnap t8nitta aligek wli klamiozw8gan, k8dak waji kiwibiamek, tkasmimek, 8mamek, lintomek ta pemeg8mek. Ni kanwa kid8benna Chila 8nda wgezaldam8wen t8nitta aligek wiag8wzow8gan. Agma pita wbalinamen wnizwidiji wedladakaw8gan ni s8gawi adoji kwagudji wl8mawaldamikh8d aliba paami wligek oji m8jin8yu, ni wdelosson8 Abitibi. Soli8n 8nda'ni wgezaldamownap lidah8zw8gan waji toji n8wosamek ta wawaldamnap ali wnizwidiji kadawi m8jida wibiwitta 'ni kw8gwnaw8gan alaklegod ta 8nda kdak kawi, Ni kanwa oji ali kzalm8d; ali kadawi wli llih8d ta kza8zwhikadaw8d 8nda wdazmowen wdelosan. Ni kaala wm8jin8 ta weli pay8n8 Abitibi. Ni kanwa nidali achi wz8malok wskinossak ni s8gawi adoji almakannidit lli nopaiwi kpiwi, t8niba 8nda awanihi adali wanask8godikw. Kw8gwnas askwa sawi wdamidah8zo kagnaba awani wdali pay8n wigw8mek, kwani 8nda aikw, n8dadialiji. Ni wdihl8n wniswdiji kam8ji saagat nmadamalsi ni 8ndaba ngizi nadialiwen. Ni Soli8n wdidamen kam8ji saagat kanwa akwi pal8balda ngiziji nia nadiali ni kia yu kdain.

Nitta kaala wn8dadialin ta wlalmekw. W8wsp8zaki wji wakassogwniwi n8dadialo ta waj8nmop wl8maw8gan waji psanilaw8t ta w8wig8dak. Nigakiwa Kw8wnas aladah8bit 'ni ni adoji m8ja wagaw8wzit ta chilait ni kwaguahliwi adoji idak: "Ndidam kbedgibna lli Abitibi saba sp8zwiwi". Soli8n idam "Kaguessaba waji pedgiakw nikw8bi niagaki yonwigi ain". Kw8wnas lli 8zidawa Wz8miga ato kwiag8wzi nspiwi awani kdak. Ni Soli8n adoji ms8dwat idak: Oh! ni kaguessi wan8daminaw8gan ni sibiwi mamhlawi mamessan8bdalmit. Kw8gwnas 8nda wgezaldamownap Soli8n alt8gwzit kanwa, wel8mastaw8, ni wdalmi ain8 ni askwa makaiwi ni wskinosis'ni wdali Aln8bain ali wihl8diji Wal8ba oji ali wl8baid ta llauk8m8d wnonona.

Kw8gwnas nitojiwi kaala sazm8wzo ta kaala 8nda kizi alokawi ni ayag8 Soli8n mina nadialit waji kiz8wzidit, waiji kagaswidah8zo ta waiji wlalmekw, abguachi p8widah8zo. Nigaki Kw8gwas adoji m8ja moskwaldak ta 8zhagadakat. T8-ni asp8dwat idak: "Niga nia n'm8ja mina n'adialin saba." Ni Soli8n wdihl8n "Kaguessa llawakan, paamat koli nanawaĭ-mezin waji 8nda kin8gui Chit8iwi almi akwamalsiwan. Wsp8-zi m8jo achakwiwik 8nda kanwa sipkossawi, ni wbadon wios ta agmatta wgissemen sibiwi walitokw klibi ta ab8na adali kissit squeda'ipeguik. Ni niziwitta welidbi mitsin8. Soli8n idam asma aguan wdidtoji wlipiwn8 tali kpiwi. Kw8gwnas 8nda wdihl8wnap Soli8na kawini kizi mijidit, ayag8tta nadod-m8god ni wdihl8n. Ennagani k'kezaldami kid8bassis awassos wiossem kizi mijiakw. 8nda ato kdillaldamowza aliji mskaok, 8h! Pasguedaga n'nossokamen al8ptowan, ni knamihollen adali saptah8an kehi tmanakw nspiwi abazi, ni awassos w'oji pn8dawan ni kd8talbapin8 kik, lli m8lami chigitolakw oji ali wdamidah8mok chijis nagalok ngwichiwi k8gawit. Ni nikw8bi kowaw8dokawlen aliba 8nda mina papiwwan spiwi awassos. Ni Soli8n wdoji moskwaldamen ta wdoji pal8bal-damen waji wibiwi m8mlisch8d. Ni kanwa n8n8gaiwi wdihl-8n, "Kwogwas ni tabat nia wji kia n'oz8mi nia majigi waji wijihlamok sassaginno, ni nikw8bitta knegallelen niji kd8t-bin8ssinta kia ta kdaw8ssizem.

Wji Tabaldak wizw8gan idam Kw8gwnas t8niba nd8lli kizi nanawalm8n kedm8gi Wal8ba. Ni Soli8n adoji mina mlisch8d kakinaw8t wnam8zsiza ni wdidamen 8ndaba kenin-gallelo kedm8gi Wal8ba, amanta waijiwi wijihlama8n knonon.

Chila, niga s8gawi nitta kmejinana ni kanwa angittaji paya8gua awaok niji nia nspiwi Wal8ba n'm8jin lli n'dadanek Chila kdelliwlaldamen ni 8h88 ala 8nda? 8h88, idam Chila ayag8ga. Niga kaala Soli8n ta wnam8zsiza wbay8n8 yo Al-sig8tekw ok.

Nag:—8h! Nzasis kizi nawa Soli8n paya Enna nawa ato yo al8jmit kassi kiz8dokawian?

Moz:—8h88 ni kanwa askwa kdak kawi kadawi hellan talini tbelo-d8zop ta matanaskt8zop adali podawazimek. Niga ato angi nizognagad ala nsognagad kizi pay8t Sali8n ni wbay8n8 nhloak Wess8gnak. Tom8, Az8 ta Salom wikodgik kchi lloka-migzowi podawazw8gan. Niga kaala achakwiwik maahl8n. Ni wajitta m8jatak wawinawakakh8n8 yugik pilwakak. Tom8 wan8gid idam: Nijiak kwawaldamn8 ali kmaomw8gak kizi wikwnemaw8mek mziwi kass8badamodit wawlikil ta mamse-

guiwkil kial tali, Maine pita ns8n8guadossa mziwi wakwa-
ta8n8 ni s8gawi adoji pay8dit Canada waji polwawdamodit
sakp8wzow8gan ta kwawaldomn8 ali nigik Wes8gnak kadm8
gida8mgodiza tawijokamgodiza milgoodit kial waji taladia-
lidit ni abguachi wdoji wlest8wadoldin8zsa waji wnam8nw8
ta wdozw8 kotli nibawoldidit, ta mziwitta wzki aln8bak nizij-
b8dwashanik Nitojiwi t8ni adoji aik kchi awdow8ganal
W8bigijik nihl8taodidiji, Wes8gnak ta W8banakiak wijihl8diji
majimiwi pasguenok wdagokak ta8lawibatta nwedkamigzi-
dida waji 8ndo awani nhl8kw wijia ala wid8ba. Nijiaak
nikw8bi 8nda km8wigapena kanwa askwa pasguen ali wijia-
toldiakw ta wid8batoldiakw ta askwatta knossokamnanawal
n8ng8ni llagidamw8ganal.

1—Phanem 8nda chowi nanihlawadakawi ala nanihlaw-
t8gwziwi illi aimgeb.

2—Phanem wdachowi kwzilawi8 ta kitaw8 wniswidiji.

3—Phanem 8nda wdachowi ngadmowen wniswidiji
n'wigwom.

Nijiak n'waj8nmobna madw8zw8gan achowi tali mata-
naskt8zik kbodawazw8 ganw8k.

Mziwi kowawalm8w8 Chila ndaln8bamna enna nibawidit Soli8na.

Kchi s8gm8 Llobal wdoza. Yu nawa al8kwim8t Chila
wniswidiji.

Pita nabiwi kizi nibawidit ni Soli8n w'm8ja nanihlawa-
dakan ta nanihlawt8gwzin illi aiddidep wskinassak, enni 8nka
waji m8jididep lli Abitibi. 8nda kanwa paami wlidbalokawip
nidali, ni s8gawi nopaiwi kpiwi wm8jin8 enni aidit sipkiwi.

Ni salikwi Soli8n n8dadialit ni Chila wnassaw8pl8n ta
wmeskaw8 adalbapidit awassossa ni wibiwitta 'ni ali ll8do-
kaw8t ni Soli8n nspiwi wnam8nsiza wm8jin lli wdadanek.

Nijiak 8ttali piwsessek kizi lli wikodmaw8mek phanem
oji ali 8nda nossokamok yulil n8ng8ni llagidamw8ganal, wm8-
jin ta w'wijhlam8n wniswi diji ta achi 8nda t8m8 wdelossa-
wen adali maahl8mek p8bapami adalga dimek wji ngueji-
gadnowaiwi 8nda awakakwa pilwi msizekw. Ni nawa ali wikodmak ta ndeli nkawadsibna aliji wli ntonguag. Ni Chaga
8nda, ninawa kdakwi lli ntoninana ta8lawi kid8baw8k ta

kijiaw8k ni wdosaigeshanna awado8gan oji ali azamakw yu
sassagak ali wikodmak kiow8jittani kedelalokaw8ganw8—
W8banakiak h8, h8, h8, h8.

Niwa kchai W8banaki'i s8gm8 wdidamen niona W8ba-
nakiak wibiwitta ndebaskodonana ma8waik oji kast8gwzi-
mek kanwa n'ngal8mlomen aliwa nid8ba Tom8 nt8wat
8lawiki p8biswi kwanataga kassi klozit. Nikw8bi kowawia-
doln8 nid8bak Wes8gnak ta W8banakiak aliji mina saba
maahl8mek niz8mkipodaga kizi paskwak niji'na wlest8wadwi
wdam8gan paswen wajiji attassi pasgo Wes8gna ta W8banaki
kizi pasgueda wikwalap8d kissed8wadimga, ni chaga 8nda
kissed8wadiwen nigaji W8banakiak wdalkwazoldin8 ta azit-
ta pasgo wdagam8n ska8gonna spiwi wdemhiganis niji oji
san8bak ta phanemok wnawadwan8 ta wbemekhedin8. Ni
achakwiwik ntami s8gm8 Llobal wm8jassadon podawazw8-
gan idak nijiak ta nid8bak oji ali'na nia ndoz Soli8n achowi
tbelom8mek yu adali podawazimek 8ndaba ma8win8guadowi
nia ntamabi8na ninawa kisn8natch awani waji n8pkawit,
t8na 8nda all8gomgowak ta 8nda allagok8kw nionak ni Pol
Sozap mam8wiwi kisn8n.

Pol Sozap kalol8d Wes8gna wdihl8: Nijiak Tom8, Az8
ta Salom, wli wawtam8nakdel8kwim8w8 Soli8n ali 8nda
nossokamok n8ng8ni llagidamw8ganal, 8nda nanh8gignowi
ll8kidw8gan, Soli8n kanwa idam ali wniswi diji lliwaldam-
lid waji yu makaiwi n8ji ait wmit8gwsek nigaki mziwi
agwjatak wdigaw8damen, ni nawa nid8banawak 8nda waj8n-
mowakw paami wligek wawizw8gan 8ndaba ngizi llalokaw-
nana ali wikodmawiak kanwa ndeli nkawatsibna aliba 8nda
wdosainok pali wawt8wadwogan ala apchik8wadw8gan oji
akw8bi 8zidawaak. Ni Az8 8zidawat wdidamen nid8banawak
ta nijianawak W8banakiak nbesani wlilawak8gonana kz8-
baski podawaswmnonw8 kz8baskid8bai podawaswinnomw8
Pol Sozap ali matanasktigat taaga achi n'oji wawisinana
agmatta Soli8n akw8bi wawiadok wzaag8wzow8gan ittoji
m8jiididep lli Abitibi ta nol8mawaldama nana ali llak mziwi
kassi idak. Kw8gwnas toji kw8gwasko waji agma nguichiwi
8nimguezit oji mziwi w'wagaw8wzow8ganw8.

Nid8bamnawag ta nijianawag idam Salom Niona Tom8,
Az8 ta nia kbakaldamikholnana ali Wes8gnak ta W8banakiak
8ndaba palsed8wadidikw ni adoji mziwitta awani k8g8lwat
ni kizi wdamhedimek ni llint8zo ta pmekhedin kwanidbakak.

NAGAKO AND MOZIS

Nag:—Uncle Mozis did you ever know an Indian named Chila or Kw8gwnas?

Moz:—Yes, nephew, an Algonquin Indian. He was so called for being cross and jealous. He married Soli8n, the daughter of Head Chief Llobal. She was considered verry pretty, good-looking and inetlligent. She was fond of good amusements such as paddling a conoe, swimming, fishing, singing and dancing but our friend Chila cared not for any kind of pleasure making. He was very displeased with his wife's manners and he tried to convince her that it would be better for them to leave this place for Abitibi. Soli8n did not like the idea of going so far and she knew that her husband was prompted to go by jealousy and nothing else, however, she did not refuse to go because she loved him and wanted to be good and kind to him. They left and happily reached Abitibi. There were too many young fellows there also, so they went on farther into the woods where no one would ever meet them, but Kw8gwnas even there was sometimes uneasy lest someone might come to his wigwam while he was out hunting. One day he told his wife: "It is too bad, I am not feeling well and cannot go hunting." Soli8n said "It is too bad, but be not discouraged, I can hunt and you stay here." She started immediately and was successful. She went out every morning for a few days and had reason to be glad and satisfied. Kw8gwnas noticing this apparent satisfaction became impatient, fretful and restless. He suddenly exclaimed: "I say we are going back to Abitibi to-morrow morning." Soli8i said, "Why should we go back now, I like to stay here?" "Yes," he said, "It may be because you have much pleasure with some one." "Oh, my what silliness!" exclaimed Soli8n and she laughed aloud disdainfully. Kw8gwnas did not like his wife's expression though it convinced him that she was right.

They stayed there for some time and a boy was born to them. His name was Wal8ba because he was handsome and resembled his mother.

The state of Health of Kw8gwna was now really poor and he was really unable to work this time. Soli8n again had to provide for their living by hunting. She was courageous and her efforts were always blessed with success and she was jovial. Kw8gwnas was indignant and acted queerly.

He spoke loudly and said: "To-morrow you stay here and I will go hunting myself." Soli8n said: "Why should you go so soon, you had better take good care of yourself so as to avoid getting worse." He left early the next morning and was not gone long. He brought a piece of meat and fried it himself; he also made some gravy and baked bread in ashes. They both ate with hearty appatite. Soli8n declared that this was the best meal they had had in the woods. Kw8gwnas did not tell her what they had eaten until she asked what it was. "Well Dear," he said, "It is the flesh of your dear friend, the bear. You never imagined that I could get at him, eh! I once followed your tracks and saw you hitting a big stub with a stick. This bear came down and played with you so long that I had to let you for the sake of the child I left at home asleep. Now let me tell you that this gambol will not be repeated, not with this bear anyway." Soli8n was so angry and abashed that she only cried and cried. After a while she said to him, "I am nothing to you after this. I am leaving you right now and you must take care of yourself and the baby." "For God's sake" said Kw8gwnas, "how could I keep the baby with me?" Soli8n looking at her little boy began to cry again and said, "I will never forsake you dear child. May you be always with your mother." "Well then Chila we will all go right away but as soon as we get out of the woods, I, with Wal8ba will go to my father's. Do you agree to this Chila, Yes or No?" "Yes, because I have to," said Chila. Soli8n and her little boy reached St-Francis all right.

Nag:—Oh! Uncle then Soli8n is at home and has told the news about herself which you have related to me.

Moz:—Yes, but what further information I mean to give you about this matter was the subject treated and settled by the Council. It was only two or three days after Soli8n came home when three Algonquins, Tom8, Az8 and Salom also arrived. They called a meeting of the tribe in Council to deal with the inter-tribal affairs. The meeting took place the next day. The three delegates were introduced to the assembly. Tom8 got up and said: "My friends and brothers you are aware no doubt that your forefathers after being deprived of their great and beautiful territories, were in great danger of annihilation in the State of Maine. They came to Canada to escape a terrible blow and it was the Algonquins who sympathized with them and gave them part of their hunting grounds. The sons and daughters of both parties intermarried and

spoke indifferently the language of either party. In time of
great wars, that is between different white nations, our ances-
tors, if they took part, were always together as of one tribe,
in order not to kill a brother or friend. Brothers, we are not
now so close together personally, but we remain brothers
and intimate friends and still follow our old regulations
in spirit, at least. Brothers, please let me refer you to the
following regulations:—

    1—a woman must not behave indecently in public.
    2—A woman must not use immoral language.
    3—A woman must respect and obey her husband.
    4—A woman must not leave the domicile of her husband.

Brothers, we have a grievance which must be settled in
your general assembly. You all know Chila, one of ours, who
married Soli8n, daughter of your head-chief Llobal. This is
Chila's accusation against his wife. Soon after they were
married she behaved indecently and spoke immorally in the
presence of young men. On account of her bad conduct they
removed to Abitibi but she behaved no better there. He next
took her far away in the woods where they lived a long time.
There a boy was born to them. One day while his wife had
gone out hunting he followed her tracks and found her play-
ing with a big bear and when he told her of this she left him
and went back to her father's.

Brothers, the least retribution that can be exacted from
a woman, for the violation of the above regulations, is to
return to and live with her husband and not attend any pu-
blic meeting especially at the dancing place, without wearing
the traditional "mask" for a term of one year. This, therefore, is our request which, we trust, is agreeable to you. If
not, than you renounce our friendship and brotherhood
and you alone will be responsible if a war follows the rejec-
tion of our just demand."

The Abenakis murmur h8, h8, h8. The old Abenaki Chief
then said: "We the Abenakis take a note only of the important things mentioned in a speech, but I admit that my friend
Tom8 is a good speaker though his speach is unnecessarily
long. I will now inform you, my friends, the Algonquins and
the Abenakis, that there will be another meeting of the Council to-morrow afternoon at two o'clock and the pipe of peace
will be brought in order that every one, Algonquin and Abenaki may draw a puff, if we come to an agreement.

If we can't agree, the Abenakis will blow their horns and each one will hit the post with his tomahawk and then all take part in the war dance."

The next day the meeting was opened by the Head Chief Llobal. After a while he said, "Because it is my daughter Soli8n who is at stake in this meeting, it is not proper for me to preside over this Council, therefore, another Councillor, one who is not related to us nor of the same party with us, must be appointed to fill this position." Pol Sozap was at once appointed accordingly. He, speaking to the three Algonquins, said: "My friends and brothers, Tom8, Az8 and Salom, if I understand rightly, you accuse Soli2n of having violated the regulations. The accusation is of momentous import. Soli8n says that with the consent of her husband she has come to stay a while with her father and denies everything else. So, dear friends, unless you can substantiate your accusation we cannot comply with your request, but we sincerely hope that no misunderstanding or trouble will arise from this our decision. Az8 replied: "Our friends and brothers the Abenakis, we are more than satisfied with the decision of your just and noble man Pol Sozap, by the bye we have also heard the version of Soli8n herself telling about her troubles and hardships while living with her husdand and we beleive that she said nothing but the truth. Kw8gwnas is so jealous that he alone is to blame for their trouble.

"Friends and brothers," said Salom, "we Tom8, Az8, and myself do promise you that there will be no trouble between the Algonquins and the Abenakis." No sooner was this said then every one shouted and after smoking the pipe of peace they all began to sing and dance all night.

XII

AZ8 LOGEN TA WZIZWIDIJI MALI NODEN

Niga agua salaqiwi saag8wzow8ganik yudali Plassowa'i Sibok, ni Az8 Logen Wsbanaki ta wnizwidiji Mali Noden, W8linaki wm8jin8ssa laguiwi Padisk8ntekwog kizi kam8ji nibek ni agua kizi sawi pmakannidid pla t8m8 wdali 8dabin8 ni agua'ni msaldozsa adbimnal wali kizadstagil ni aganaga nillil mijidit wz8miga kadoposhanik ni illi mijididep adbimnal ni niziwitta agm8w8 wnamih8n8 moza ay8ba patkwag8bit yutta pamibizagassik nik8nik8niwi agm8w8k ni 8nda w'waldamown8 t8niba wdelalokan8 waji kizi nhl88dit wz8-

miga Az8 8nda wgizi mskamownal w'mamsagmal niga s8gawi adoji
mliki pitkazawat wbaskigan nspiwi adbimen'i paknemal sibiwi
pask8t moza wdebek, Mozgaki wibiwitta nanamaskwamdam ni
wd8lemi m8manni m8jin. Ni s8gawi achi agm8w8 Az8 ta Mali adoji
almakannidit ni Az8 wdihl8n wnizwidiji kam8ji owa moz kd8zha-
gikad8gonna 8h88 idam Mali kanwa 8ndaganna moz mdawleno-
gana. Mdawleno! idam Az8. Mdawlenoak wdain8 kia wajiawian?
8h88 idam Mali wdainga pazgo kanwa 8nda kawilli 8zhagi wagalo-
kawi. Tbaskozi knamitoji kagui askwa paami 8zhagilawak8gwan
asma mina namitowan Plaswa'i sibo. Ni wdali pebonamin8'ni t8m8
laguiwi ta wdain8 askwa lli kam8ji nibek ni oji wbedginn8 ta
wnosokamen8 wadagossadidep taaki wdali pay8n8 adali namih8-
didep moza ni kawi aiga, abguachi paami msaldol ta paami
wlignol adbimnal 8ndaki ni akw8baiy8l. Ni 8zoka'ni paki lli
8tsapskassigi ni Az8 adali mijik ta adali mawizit adbimnal ni Mali
agma ait kik wnodawun Az8a K8gslwad; Mali, Mali ni Mali nem8 alih-
l8t kizi ndat8m8 8tsapskassik ta enna Albimnakwan adalawizidep
Az8 achi ndat8m8 nigaki agmatta Az8 wd8dolessinnen'ni kik paki
machinawinno. Ni Mali adoji awskapol8t sibiwi ahl8t Az8 Az8 kawi
kdezi, nigaki adoji 8mikit Az8 ni wnami8n8 moza ta adbinakwamma
wajigit wdaskanikok. Ni kizimoz almi miwosat wnodaw8n8 awanihi
idak Mali Mali Az8 Mali Az8 Loden Noden.

Ni agua Mali wdihl8n wnizwidiji ni nikw8bi knamitum kizi
llalokat mdawleno.

ST-FRANCIS INDIAN RESERVE, P. Q.

Once upon a time it was hard to make a living here. John
Loden, Abenaki Indian and his wife Mali Nigen, a Wawenock of
Becancour, P. Q. left rather late in summer and went towards Ba-
tiscan River near Rat River, P. Q.

One day, after a long walk, being tired and hungry, they stopped at a certain place to have a rest and there saw a large quantity
of ripe cherries and while they were eating some they both saw
a bull moose standing behind a little bush facing them. They did not
know what to do to kill him because John could not find his musket
balls and so he loaded his gun heavily with cherry stones and shot
him on the head, but that did not take effect, as he only shook his
head and slowly went away.

John and Mary continued on their journey. John told his
wife:—"This moose has acted queerly with us." "Yes." said Mary,
"but he is not a moose, he is a sorcerer." "A sorcerer!" said John:

"Are there any sorcerers at the place you are from?" "Yes," said Mary, "There is one but he does not cause much damage mysteriously. Remark what I say: Thou shalt see something more wonderful than this ere thou again comest to St-Francis River."

They spent the winter thereabouts and remained there until the latter part of the summer, when they started to come back and followed the way they had gone thither. They at last reached the place where they had seen a moose, and, if anything the cherries were better and in greater quantity than the year before. There was something new and peculiar in the place, it was a small elevation as it seemed of rock and the shape of a gourd. It was there where John was eating and picking cherries and Mary, who was on the lower ground, heard John calling, "Mary, Mary," and Mary ran to him but ha! the elevation had disappeared and the cherry-tree, from which John was picking cherries, had also faded away, and as to John himself, he was on the ground lying on his back and looked like a corpse.

Mary shook him, rapidly saying: "John, John, what is the matter with you?" John recovered consciousness and got up on his feet, just then the moose was walking away with the small elevation and the big cherry-tree on his back and horns; at the same time John and Mary heard some one say: "Mary, Mary, John, Mary, Mary, John Loden, Mary Nigen."

After everything was over Mary said to her husband: "You see now what a sorcerer can do." "Yes," said John, "but it is so amazing that I can hardly believe it."

XIII

KAZIHL8T

Niga agua pasgueda kazihl8t ta wnizwidiji Malian niziwita yo Alsig8ntekwog ojiawinn8zsa ni kanwa kizi wakassigaden wnoji ainn8zsa Mad8balodnitekw-og ni 'ni wdali wijihlamgon8zsa wski aln8ba aliwizit Mikm8z wjia (Acadia,) ni 8zoka Kazihl8t kizinolhamossa wji ligadmaw8gan ni 8nda kagwi wdel8bamgueziwen aiyag8 waiji nodn8mek ta lli nanawalm8mek ta8lawitta aw8zsis, pajiga aiyag8 pon8mek tkin8ganek waji kizi wli kawit ni noskiwi wgizi lli wl8mawaldamighozin ali kala agma aw8zsis, aliji mina wskinoswit ta mina nibawit; ni Malian tagdatta wdalmi 8lawitun oji adoji saakat; ni 8lawi wigaw8jiwi wigt8gwzow8damen wajiba m8jidit lli Alsig8ntekw-og paki Kazihl8t 8nda amojka nodamokwi id8zik; ni 8soka wgini wl8mawaldamnashanil lekwsow8ganal, majimiwi, wgadawi wawaldamnap t8ni kdagik alguassidit; ni'na Mikm8z mziwi kagui wd8dbaskozin, ni salakiwi adoji kimiwi hl8nt Malianna: "Nwawaldamen nia t8niba chowi lli kadaw8n Kazihl8t waji kizi nodak ta wowtak kagwi alh8mek, niba oji, 8ndaba wibiwitta wdeli wlaldamowen km8jinana lli Odanak, kanwa agmattaba'ni kdelagimgonana wiwhiz8iwi," ni Malian odidamen. "Kaguessa nawa'ni wawaldaman adojiba wl8bamguak?" Ni Mikm8z wdihl8n, "8ndagaba kgizi hlellowen nikw8bi; kanwaba ngizitun idama lli wlaldamana." Ni phanemwdidamen ni atokaala ndeli wlaldamen taaji 8nda kodaldamowen ni kizitwana, wibiwitta akwi 8ntalli 8ttokan, wz8mi akw8bi nabiwi niji akw8bi wligek wji kia ta nia." ni achakwiwik, ta8lawitta w8wsp8zaki, Kazihl8t wdihl8n Mikm8za, "Kagui nawa kdelgassi pamidbakak?" Ni Mikm8z wdhl8n:" Niga asma wad8wzia ndoji majguassiwen, abguachiga 8nda ngadawi wawiadowen."

Kazihl8t:—Kanwagakiba kdachowi kin8gwi nia hlin, wz8mi waijiwitta kdi hlin alguassian, niba kaguessa nikw8bi waji 8nda?

Mikm8z:—Niga s8gawi kdil hlen: "Ndelguassiga ali sp8zwiwi pab8mwi n8n8mki podak pab8mi kiossaa yo laguiwi almadnikak, ni'ni ndali wanaskaw8n san8ba, oji akw8bin8gwzit pab8miwi ato n8nninska kassigadema kanwa kagasgamto ta, matanaski wlidbin8gwzo ta achi wilawigwin8gwzo, ni n'nadodm8gun t8ni yo nia ndeli ojiawin ni ndi hl8n ali 8nda kanwa ali kizi kwinatta n8wat n'oji aiya; Ni wdidamen: Kwawinaw8k nawa ato Kazihl8t ta wnizwidiji Malian? Ennaga kedm8gi maji sazig8damwinno kizi nanni kwaskwi mamagah8t wnizwidiji ni kanwa tabat almiji ngalgot Malianna 8ndali mina wnamih8wia." Ni oji Mikm8z nde lekwsow8ganek enna ma8wi san8ba mina w'nami8 al8msagog nspiwi phanem alinaw8ji ta8lawi Malian. Ni noli k8kani tokin. "Akwi kigui idamokan"

Ni achakwiwik, angitta al8bak, Kazihl8t wgek8g8lwan, Malian, Malian nab8ji km8jibna Alsig8ntekw-og pami sp8zwik. 8nda sipkin8gwadowi ni gizi Malian wgiz8jin. Ni angitta kizi sp8zipidit kaala wm8jin8. 8nda kinni sipkiwi kizi pay8dit Alsig8ntekw-og ni Kazihl8t wmatanaskihl8n.

KAZIHL8T

Once upon a time, Kazihl8t and his wife, Marion, who originally were from St-Francis River Reserve, stayed for many years at St-Maurice River. There a young Indian of Acadia, Mikm8z by name, lived with them.

Kazihl8t seemed to be unable to do any work, owing to old age, he had to be constantly attended to by his wife, and the poor woman spent more time on him than if he were a child; she often had to give him a good bath and then put him in bed to sleep. He imagined or believed that he had become, really a child and that he would grow to be a young man and marry again.

Marion was so exhausted by her troubles and hard work that, she often insinuated that they should return to St-Francis River Reserve. Kazihl8t was deaf to what she said. However he was a firm believer in dreams; he always wanted to know the dreams of other people.

Mikm8z always observed the things going on. He one day, told Marion secretly: "I know how Kazihl8t should be dealt with to make him hear and understand any thing said to him, and after that, he would not only let us go to Odanak, but he himself would tell us to make haste to go there." Marion then said to Mikm8z: "What is that, that you know to be so helpful?" Mikm8z answered: "I cannot tell you now but with your permission will do as I said." The woman replied: "You will not be sorry for it, only do not put it off, because the sooner it is done the better it will be for you and me."

The next morning, as habitually every morning, Kazihl8t said to Mizm8z: "What did you dream last night?" Mikm8z replied: "I never had such a bad dream in all my life and I prefer not to say any thing about it."

Kazihl8t:—You should let me know it, since you have nevr refused me any thing, and why should you do so now?

Mikm8z:—You are right, well then: I dreamt that one day early in the morning at about five o'clock, as I was taking a walk toward the mountains, I met a man about fifty years of age, who was very lively, he looked fine and rich. He asked me if I belonged to this place. I said: "No but have lived here for years." Then said he: "You perhaps know Kazihl8t and his wife, Marion. He is the lazy devil who has ill treated his poor wife nearly to death, but this is the end of ill treatement. Marion is to leave him and he will never see her again."

In my dream, I again saw the man in a room with a woman whom I thought was Marion, but was not sure.

I am now wide awake. Say nothing about my dream. The next morning at dawn, Kazihl8t cried out: "Marion, Marion, make haste, we are going to Alsig8ntekw og this morning." She got ready in a very short time and they all left right after breakfast. Not very long after they reached Alsig8ntekwog, Kazihl8t passed away.

XIV

WIJOKAMIT TA MA8WAT

Wij:—Kwai, Kwai, nad8gues kam8ji nwig8dam namiholan, kizi yu n8wat kojim8jin.

Ma8:—8h88, niga kizi t8baw8z kassi gaden ni ndelidah8zin wji kizi kassigadmaa pami wligen wji nia nm8jin Alsig8ntekwog niga 8zoka wajiawia.

Wij:—Nad8gues ni kdali wl8man. Kgassigadema pgua?

Ma8:—Niga kizi t8baw8z kassinska taba n8lan.

Wij:—Nad8gues nia nawa nbami kchiawi 8ndaki kia, kizi nia t8-baw8z kassinska taba noliwi ngassi gadema. Nad8gues kwigiba nadodmol kagui.

Ma8:—Nadodmawiga wz8mi 8nda kawi ndelaloka nikw8bi.

Wij:—Nigakdilhlen kanwa tagasiwi kwn8baga. Pab8miwi mdala kassi gadmaa nwijaw8p Lol8 Tam8da n8ji moskwassokat ni attassiwi kizi adl8guipiagi nd8dokawgon kagui n8ng8niwi alakep. Lol8 nitojiwi ns8zek kassinska taba pazekw kassi gadmap ni yu 8dokawidep wdelsedaw8naza wmahoma, ninawa wlidbiwi nizategua kassi gaden yu llassa kadawi 8dokawlan. Nijia yu nikw8bi ali wit8zik Odanak kiona 8pchi aiyakw ni achi agm8w8 aidiza waj8nmoshanik wakasnol abazigamigwol ta massalkil maskwa'ik8nal ni agua salakiwi kini pmekhedin ta kadosmoldin ni agua adalg8mek wdalipayon kchi wdowi awanoch ni platta ntami wibiwitta tbinasso ni oji wwikodmen waji achi agma widg8t. 8zoka toji kwzilawakamigzo waji 8ndaba kizi aza8mmok ni kanwa wibiwtta kwina phanemo walikadaw8ji wgelol8gaki achi san8ba kanwa wibiwitta waji kizi kagazwah8t wg8gadosmoldin8, ni k8dak nodalhl8k akwbi nitta wmagan m8ni waji mina nimsk8zik lli ag8mek, ali wit8zik, San Plassowa. agma kanwa 8nda kwina wejesmiwen ni mina wdihl8n nodhebaliji mina nimska akwbi, ni Sozap, nodhebat, wdidamen "8nda t8m8 m8ni" ni owa wdidamen, "Nimskadaki akwbi askwa kwaj8nem m8ni kbid8ganek." Sozap alinskat wbid8ganek, kaliki askwa ao m8ni, ni oji kwanitbakak awatheba, ta attassi wmachimagan wm8nim ni kanwatta mina n8bi llimijbo wbid8gan. Ni agua nanni achakwak askwa owa wdowiawanoch pab8mtakak nspiwi papsigagihl8nk wbidk8zon ni ni wewji s8khiazo wzogwna, ni phanemok ta gattaachi san8bak wdidamen8, Madah8ndogawa. Askwa ali kinaw8dit sakat, ni illi g8bidep wdeliakwi namiguezin.

Ni nikw8bi Nad8gues, nwigiba wawaldamen t8niwa madah8ndo, ali wihl8mek, wdeli kizi milzin llin8gzow8gan t8nittayu achwaldak ta t8ni lli kawi ao t8niba kizi wji wawinaw8mek?

Ma8:—Wijokagamit, niga kdilhlen akw8bi nia wowtama: Madah8ndo kizi milzo linogwzow8gan t8nitta aligek ta achi l8dwaw8gan wajikiziwnemih8t wzidkamiguinnoa. Wgizik8dak milzinnap whelin8gwzow8gan skok ta laguidah8mguat ali ato pita wli n8gwziza skok asma majalmegok Tabaldamliji kw8gwnibgua kizi wnemih8t ntami phanemo. Ni agua n8bi wgizi llin8kwzik hozinaza ta8lawi wawassi pessakwlanigani 8zaliak spemkik aidjik wgizi kwaguaji wnemih8zhani t8nba wz8miga wnalawi achi llosanaza spemkik lli m8lami kz8gm8mna Sazos kizi 8mbijibat ta pay8t spemkik.

Madah8ndo na niwaskw ni 8zoka niwaskw 8nda whagaiwi, 8nda nawa achi wdaskaniwi, ala psigikazawi, ta 8nda wzognaiwi, kanwa wgizi tun waji llin8gwzit, ta8lawi pm8wzowinno, ta8lawi awas ala nidazo, ni nawa namih8mga pm8wzowinno wdaskanit ala wzognait kiziba wl8ma id8zo ali na Madah8ndo.

WIJOKAMIT AND MA8WAT

Wij:—Hallo! Hallo! Cousin Ma8wat how glad I am to se you. You have been away quite a while.

Ma8:—Yes, it is seven years since I left this place and I thought, old as I am, it would be better for me to return to St-Francis, that is where I belong anyway.

Wji:—Cousin what you say is right. How old are you?

Ma8:—I am past seventy-five years of age.

Wij:—Cousin, then I am older than you. I am seventy-nine years old. Cousin I would like to ask you something.

Ma8:—Say what you want, I am not busy now.

Wij:—Well, then I must first tell you my story though it is a little bit long. When I was about ten years of age, I went with Lol8 Ta8mont muskrat hunting and every day after supper he would tell me things of old. He was then eighty-one years old, so the things referred to must have taken place two hundred years ago. Our forefathers lived and died at this place where we are living, now called Odanak. They owned a few houses and many birch-back wigwams. Once upon a time, while they were dancing and drinking (Akwbi) "bitter-water" rum, a white man of great nobility came in there and for some time only observed the place and people, but at last asked permission to dance with them. He was so polite that they could not refuse to allow him to dance with them, but they soon remarked that he paid special attention to the women; when he spoke to the men it was only to encourage them in their frolic and drinking. For instance as soon as they were short of liquor he furnished the money for some more from St-François, across the river, but he did not drink much of it himself, and when that was all gone too, he told the man to go for some more liquor, and Joseph who used to get it said, "We have no money," and the gentleman said to him, "Make haste and get some more whiskey, you have some money in your pocket." And Joseph did truly find some in his pocket, and after that he got some more and more all night long, and strange to say, his pocket was never empty when he came back though it took all he had each time to pay for the liquor.

At dawn of the day the noble white man was still dancing with his coat on, something like a Prince Albert coat and through the slit the women and the men too, saw his tail and all said he is the devil, and while looking at him, he slowly disappeared.

Now, Cousin, I would like to know if the devil, as we call him, can assume any human form or the likeness of anything he chooses and whether there is something by means of which we can detect him?

Ma8:—Wijokamit, I will tell you my impression of the case. The devil can assume human form, animal form, and the likeness of anything. He can also speak any language to tempt persons and nations of the world. For instance he assumed the form of an animal when he tempted Eve in the garden of Eden. The looks of the serpent must have been very pleasing before his fall, since he succeeded in deceiving the first woman. He not only assumed the animal form, but he transformed himself into an angel of light and went to heaven to tempt the holy angels. He was allowed to go there until the resurrection and ascension of our Lord, Jesus Christ.

The devil is a sperit and a sperit has no flesh nor bone, it follows that he has no horns, no cloven hoofs, and no tail, but he can make himself to look like a person, like a beast, etc., so if a person is seen having horns or tail, we may say assuredly,—"he is the devil."

PART II

ABENAKI INDIAN GRAMMAR

PARTS OF SPEECH

There are eighe parts of speech:—

Noun, Adjective, Pronoun, Verb, Adverb, Preposition, Conjunction and Interjection.

CLASSIFICATION OF NOUNS

Nouns are divided into two principal classas:—

1—Strong Nouns.
2—Weak Nouns.

Strong Nouns are subdivided into Proper Nouns.
Weak Nouns are subdivided into Abstract Nouns.

STRONG NOUNS

Strong Nouns are the names of persons, animals, birds, fishes, insects, and of all living things including trees, of celestial bodies as the sun, moon and stars, of things cheerful and awful in the sky, as the Rainbow, and Thunder, of things high and grand on earth as the mountains, etc.

WEAK NOUNS

Weak nouns are the names of inanimate things, of some plants, weeds, and small fruits.

PROPER NOUNS

A proper noun is a name given to some particular person, place or thing, i. e.

Az8, John, Molian, Montreal.

ABSTRACT NOUNS

An abstract noun is the name of a quality or action or a state of being, i. e.

Wlin-no "wg"—*goodness,* nadial "wg"—*hunting,* wli-to-dab "wg"—*well being.*

PROPER NOUNS

Molian—*(Montreal.)*
N'Kebak—*(Quebec.)*
Paliten—*(Burlington.)*

Salatogi—*(Saratoga.)*
Milwaigki—*(Milwaukee.)*

ABSTRACT NOUNS

Aln8baw8gan—*Birth.*
Alokaw8gan—*Work.*
Aw8zsisw8gan—*Infancy.*
Chilaw8gan—*Crossness.*
Lida8zw8gan—*Thought.*
Ligadmaw8gan—*Age.*
Lintow8gan—*Song.*

Magigw8gan—*Wickedness.*
Mlikigw8gan—*Stoutness.*
Moskwaldamw8gan—*Anger.*
Nibaw8gan—*Marriage.*
Nik8n8jmow8gan—*Prophecy.*
P8batamw8gan—*Religion.*

STRONG NOUNS

Abazi—*Tree.*
Agaskw—*Ground hog.*
Agbalam—*Bull frog.*
Ahamo—*Hen.*
Aksen—*Ox* (en)
Alakws—*Star.*
Alikws—*Ant.*
Almos—*Dog.*
Alm8zka—*Mole.*
Alnamagw—*Dace.*
Aln8ba—*Indian.*
Anibi—*Elm.*
Awak8n—*Slave.*
Awanoch—*Whiteman.*
Awaas—*Beast.*

Chanaps—*Turnip.*
Cheskwadadas—*King fisher.*
Chibai—*Ghost.*
Chogleskw—*Black bird.*
Ch8ls—*Grasshopper.*

Kaakw—*Gull.*
Kabassa—*Sturgeon.*
Kag8wakw—*Prickly ash.*
Kanozas—*Willow.*
Kaoz—*Cow.*

Kbej8las—*Conch shell.*
Kin James—*King James.*
Kik8mkwa—*Sucker.*
Kin8ba—*Brave man.*
Kizos—*Sun.*
Kokokhas—*Owl.*
Kokokh8akw—*Fir tree.*
Kotz—*Goat.*
K8gw—*Porcupine.*
Kwiguigam—*Duck.*
Kwnoza—*Pike.*

Mahlakws—*Black ash.*
Mamij8la—*Butterfly.*
Managuen—*Rainbow.*
Manistel—*Minister.*
Maska—*Toad.*
Matguas—*Rabbit.*
Mazeszakwa—*Horse-fly.*
Mdawawinno—*Complainant.*
Mhlosses—*Old man.*
Minuïs—*Kitten.*
Moskwas—*Muskrat.*
Mossagua—*Woodworm.*
Moz—*Moose.*
Mozbas—*Mink.*
Mozmen—*Moose berry.*

M8laloskw—*Lever wood.*
M8l8dakw—*Cedar.*
M8lsem—*Wolf.*
Mskask—*Spruce.*
Mzazesso—*White Spruce.*

Nah8mo—*Eel.*
Namagw—*Salmon trout.*
Namas—*Fish.*
Nodab8nkad—*Baker.*
Nodadslgad—*Dyer.*
Nodahlagokad—*Blacksmith.*
Nojikkad—*Joiner.*
Nojikz8wad—*Sawyer.*
Nojim8nikad—*Silver smith.*
Nodkeznikad—*Shoemaker.*
Nod8mad—*Fisherman.*
Nod8kwad—*Cook.*
Nodtaasid—*Miller.*
Nodtah8d—*Butcher.*
Nolka—*Deer.*
N8bahla—*Rooster.*
N8bakikw—*Male Otter.*
N8bassem—*Male beast.*

Ojawas—*Fly.*

8gmakw—*White Ash.*

Pabaskw—*Bloodsucker.*
Pabikw—*Flea.*
Pagimizi—*Walnut tree.*
Pag8nozi—*Butternut tree.*
Patlih8z—*Priest.*
Pegues—*Mosquito.*
Pequis—*Gnat.*

Pelaz—*Pigeon.*
Pezo—*Wolverine.*
Phanem—*Woman.*
Pigs—*Pig.*
Planikw—*Flying squirrel.*
P8guas—*Moon.*
Pziko—*Buffalo.*

San8ba—*Man.*
Sasasso—*Snipe.*
Sodi *Hemlock.*
Sigiliamo—*Locust.*
Sips—*Bird.*
Skog—*Snake.*
S8gm8—*Cheif.*

Wachilmezi—*White oak.*
Wajo—*Mountain.*
Wajwimizi—*Beech tree.*
Wal8yas—*Owl.*
Wanahlos—*Forgetful person.*
Wawasinno—*Saint.*
Wdopi—*Alder.*
Wigbimizi—*Basswood.*
Wiguahla—*Swan.*
Wins—*Black birch.*
Winoz—*Onion.*
Wlanikw—*Fisher.*
Wnegikw—*Otter*
W8bigihlakw—*Goose.*
W8boz—*Elk.*
W8gwses—*Fox.*
W8phagas—*Carp.*
W8zesso—*Pout.*

WEAK NOUNS

Ab8n—*Bread.*
Abon—*Bed.*
Amassol—*Wooden Conoe.*
Asolkwen—Hat.
Awan—*Air.*
Awazon—*Wood.*
Aw8gan—*Bait.*

Kalas—*Calash.*
Kik8n—*Field.*
Kizokw—*Day.*
Kl8gan—*Door.*
Ktolakw—*Ship.*
Kzel8msen—*Wind.*
Kz8bo—*Broth.*

WEAK NOUNS (*continued*)

Lal8p—*Lamp.*

Malto—*Hammer.*
Massipskw—*Flint.*
Mgoakw—*Swamp.*
Miguen—*Feather.*
Mizwa—*Dandruff.*
Mkaza—*Coal.*
Mkezen—*Shoe.*
Mkezn8bi—*Shoestring.*
Mnahan—*Island.*
Mnoda—*Bag.*
Moswa—*Shawl.*
Moz8bi—*Bead.*

Nagako—*Sand.*
Nbes—*Lake.*
Nebi—*Water.*
Nebizon—*Medecine.*
Niben—*Summer.*
Nokhigan—*Flour.*
N8pkowan—*Collar.*

Odana—*Village.*
Ol8kw—*Blue sky.*

8wan—*Egg.*
8wdi—*Road.*

Pabalhad—*Beaver hat.*
Pakwa—*Arrow.*
Paskigan—*Gun.*
Patnes—*Button.*
Pigueskw—*Spunk.*
Pik8n—*String.*
Pilaskw—*Paper.*
Piltal—*Lead.*
Podin—*Pudding.*
Pokwda—*Fire brand.*
P8ntekw—*Rapids.*

Saidal—*Cider.*
Saksahon—*Earring.*
Sen—*Stone.*
Sibo—*River.*
Sikwhla—*Hail.*
Silki—*Silk.*
Silad—*Vest.*
Siwan—*Salt.*
Skawakw—*Fresh meat.*
Skweda—*Fire*
Sobakw—*Sea.*
Sogal—*Sugar.*
Sop—*Soap.*
Spemsakw—*Up stairs.*

Talin—*Eathen basin.*
Tawz8gan—*Glass.*
Tebokw—*Night.*
Tmahigan—*Axe.*
Tossen—*Shed.*

Wagin—*Waggon.*
Waguan—*Heel.*
Walaskw—*Husk.*
Wdep—*Head.*
Wdepkwan—*Head hair.*
Wdon—*Mouth.*
Wibit—*Tooth.*
Wika—*Fat.*
Wiyos—*Meat.*
Wj8l—*Nose.*
Wlogas—*Leather string.*
W8lakw—*Hole.*
Wskadgua—*Forehead.*
Wzidakw—*Axe handle.*

NUMBER

Strong nouns form their plural by adding "ak" te the singular except a few ending in akw, skw, agw and em to which "ok" is added to the singular and "jik" to a few other words ending in ad and id.

Examples:—

Strong nouns: Singular,

> Aln8ba plus ak—*Indians.*
> Agaskw plus ok—*Woodchucks.*
> Alnamagw plus ok—*Daces.*
> Kaakw plus ok—*Gulls.*
> M8lsem plus ok—*Wolves.*
> Nod8mad plus jik—*Fishermen.*
> Nodaksid plus jik—*Sailors.*

> See the list of strong nouns.

Weak uouns form their plural by adding "al" to the singular except a few ending in kw and gw to which "ol" is added to the singular.

Examples:—

Weak nouns, Singular,

> Kask plus al—*Caps.*
> Nbes plus al—*Lakes.*
> Pneg8kw plus ol—*Sandy hills.*
> Skawagw plus ol—*Fresh meats.*

> See the list of weak nouns.

INFLECTION OF NOUNS

Nouns are inflected to mark number and case.

GENDER

Nouns are also divided into two classes or sorts callad Genders.

These are Noble Gender and Common Gender.

All Strong Nouns are of the Noble Gender.

All Weak Nouns are of the Common Gender.

The sex is designated in three ways:—

First:—By different words, i. e.

San8ba—*Man.*   Phanem—*Woman.*
Wskinnos—*Batchelor.*   N8ksqua—*Maid.*
Wskinnossis—*Boy.*   N8ksquassis—*Girl.*
Nijia—*Brother.*   Nid8pso—*Sister.*
N'dadan—*Papa.*   N'nonon—*Mother.*
N'nam8n—*Son.*   N'doz—*Daughter.*
N'nam8n'imis—*Nephew.*   N'doz'imis—*Niece.*
N'mit8gues—*Father.*   Nigawes—*Mother.*
N'mahom—*Grandfather.*   Nokemes—*Grandmother.*
N'zihlos—*Father-in-law.*   Nzegues—*Mother-in-law.*
Wazilmit—*Son-in-law.*   Nsem—*Doughter-in-law.*
N8jikw—*Stepfather.*   Nokemis—*Stepmother.*
Nad8kw—*Brother-in-law.*   Nilem—*Sister-in-law.*
Nidokan—*Elder brother.*   Nmessis—*Elder sister.*
Ndadanis—*Uncle (Father's bro-* Nnononis—*Aunt (Mother's sister)*
   ther)
Nzassis—*Uncle   (Mother's bro-* Nokem— *Aunt (Father's sister)*
   ther)

MALE	FEMALE

MOOSE

Ay8ba—*Father*   Alhla—*Mother.*
Kadnadokw—*3 years old.*   Alhlasis—
Makwses—*2 years old.*

BEAVERS

N8bamskw—*Father.*   Squamskw—*Mother.*
Piawa—*2 years old.*   Palmeskw—*2 years old.*
Awalzis—*Young.*   Awalzis—*Young.*

Second:—By different termination, i. e.

Nodalokat—*Servant.*   Nodalokasqua—*Maidservant.*
Manistel—*Minister.*   Manistel'isqua—*Minister's wife.*
Sigwid—*Widower.*   Sigosqua—*Wiow.*
Kinjames—*King.*   Kinjames'isqua—*King's wife.*

Third:—By adding a word indicating sex, i. e.

Sanoba nodalokat—*Man servant.* Phanem nodalokat—*Maid servant*
Ay8ba moz—*Bull moose.* Alhla moz—*Cow moose.*
N8bakikw wnegikw—*He otter.* Squakikw wneglkw—*She otter.*
N8bassem almos—*Male dog.* Squassem almos—*Bitch.*
N8bahla sips—*Male bird.* Squahla sips—*Female bird.*

CASE

Nouns in Abenaki have six cases:—
　Nominative, genitive, dative, accusative, vocative and ablative.

The strong nouns in Nominative Singular ending in "a"

　　Singular.　　　　　　　Plural.

Nom:—San8ba—*Man.* San8bak—*Men.*
Gen:—San8ba'i—*Man's.* San8ba'i—*Men's.*
Dat:—San8bak—*To man.* San8ba ikok—*To men.*
Acc:—San8ba—*Man.* San8ba—*Men.*
Voc:—O San8ba—*O man.* O San8bak—*O men.*
Abl:—San8bak—*From or by man.* San8bak ikok—*From or by men.*

—ending in "am"

Nom:—Scotam—*Trout.* Scotamak—*Trouts.*
Gen:—Scotam'i—*Trout's.* Scotam'i—*Trouts'.*
Dat:—Scotamek—*To trout.* Scotamikok—*To trouts.*
Acc:—Scotama—*Trout.* Scotama—*Trouts.*
Voc:—
Abl:—Scotamek—*From or by---* Scotamikok—*From or by trouts.*

—ending in "b"

Nom:—Azib—*Sheep.* Azib ak—*Sheep.*
Gen:—Azib'i—*Sheep's.* Azib'i—*Sheeps'.*
Dat:—Azib ek—*To sheep.* Azib ikok—*To sheep.*
Acc:—Azib a—*Sheep.* Azib a—*Sheep.*
Voc:—
Abl:—Azib ek—*From or by sheep* Azib ikok—*From or by sheep.*

—ending in "d"

Singular.	Plural.
Nom:—Nodalokad—*Servant.*	Nodalokad jik—*Servants.*
Gen:—Nodalokad'i—*Servant's.*	Nodalokad'i—*Of Servants'.*
Dat:—Nodalokad ek—*To Servant.*	Nodalokad ikok—*To Servants.*
Acc:—Nodalokad ji—*Servant.*	Nodalokaliji—*Servants.*
Voc:—O Nodalokad—*O Servant.*	O Nodaloka jik—*O Servants.*
Abl:—Nodalokad ek—*From or by*	Nodalokad ikok—*From or by---*

—ending in "em"

Nom:—M8lsem—*Wolf.*	M8lsem ok—*Wolves.*
Gen:—M8lsem'i—*Wolf's.*	M8lsem'i—*Wolves'.*
Dat:—M8lsem ok—*To Wolf.*	M8lsem ikok—*To Wolves.*
Acc:—M8lsem o—*Wolf.*	M8lsem ok—*Ok Wolves.*
Voc:—O M8lsem—*O Wolf.*	O M8lsem—*Ok O Wolves.*
Abl:—M8lsem ok—*From or by---*	M8lsem ikok—*From or by---*

—ending in "8z, Oz, s or ss"

Nom:—Patlih8z—*Priest.*	Patlih8z ak—*Priests.*
Gen:—Patlih8z'i—*Priest's.*	Patlih8z'i—*Priests'.*
Dat:—Patlih8 ek—*To Priest.*	Patlih8z ikok—*To Priests.*
Acc:—Patlih8z a—*Priest.*	Patlih8z a—*Priests.*
Voc:—O Patlih8z—*O Priest.*	O Patlih8z ak—*O Priests.*
Abl:—Patlih8z ek—*From or by---*	Patlih8z ikok—*From or by---*

Nom:—Awasoss—*Bear.*	Awasossak—*Bears.*
Gen:—Awasoss'i—*Bear's.*	Awasoss'i—*Bears'.*
Dat:—Awasoss ek—*To bear.*	Awasoss ikok—*To bears.*
Acc:—Awasoss a—*Bear.*	Awasoss a—*Bears.*
Voc:—O Awasoss—*O Bear.*	O Awasoss ak—*O Bears.*
Abl:—Awasoss ek—*From or by---*	Awasoss ikok—*From or by---*

Nom:—Kaoz—*Cow.*	Kaoz ak—*Cows.*
Gen:—Kaoz'i—*Cow's.*	Kaoz'i—*Cows'.*
Dat:—Kaoz ek—*To Cow.*	Kaoz ikok—*To Cows.*
Acc:—Kaoz a—*Cow.*	Kaoz a—*Cows.*
Voc:—	
Abl:—Kaoz ek—*From or by---*	Kaoz ikok—*From or by Cows.*

—ending in "i, l, kw"

Singular.	Plural.
Nom:—Titgeli—*Owl.*	Titgeli ak—*Owls.*
Gen:—Titgeli'i—*Owl's.*	Titgeli'i—*Owls'.*
Dat:—Titgeli k—*To Owl.*	Titgeli ikok—*To owls.*
Acc:—Titgeli a—*Owl.*	Titgeli a—*Owls.*
Voc:—	
Abl:—Titgeli k—*From or by---*	Titgeli ikok—*From or by owls.*
Nom:—Chegual—*Frog.*	Chegual ak—*Frogs.*
Gen:—Chegual'i—*Frog's.*	Chegual'i—*Frogs'.*
Dat:—Chegual ek—*To Frog.*	Chegual ikok—*To frogs.*
Acc:—Chegual a—*Frog.*	Chegual a—*Frogs.*
Voc:—	
Abl:—Chegual ek—*From or by---*	Chegual ikok—*From or by frogs.*
Nom:—Agaskw—*Ground hog.*	Agaskw ok—*Ground hogs.*
Gen:—Agaskw'i—*Ground hog's.*	Agaskw'i—*Grounds'.*
Dat:—Agaskw ok—*To ground hog*	Agaskw ikok—*To grond hogs.*
Acc:—Agaskw o—*Ground hog.*	Agaskw o—*Ground hogs.*
Voc:—	
Abl:—Agaskw ok—*From or by---*	Agaskw ikok—*From or by---*

WEAK NOUNS ARE DECLINED THUS

The Nominative Singular ending in "an, a, kw"

Singular.	Plural.
Nom:—Wl8gan—*Dish.*	Wl8gan al—*Dishes.*
Gen:—Wl8gan'i—*Dish's.*	Wl8gan'i—*Dishes'.*
Dat:—Wl8gan ek—*To dish.*	Wl8gan ikok—*To dishes.*
Acc:—Wlogan—*Dish.*	Wl8gan al—*Dishes.*
Abl:—Wl8gan ek—*From or by---*	Wl8gan ikok—*From or by dishes.*
Nom:—Mnoda—*Bag.*	Mnoda al—*Bags.*
Gen:—Mnoda'i—*Bag's.*	Mnoda'i—*Bags'.*
Dat:—Mnoda k—*To bag.*	Mnoda ikok—*To bags.*
Acc:—Mnoda—*Bag.*	Mnoda al—*Bags.*
Abl:—Mnoda k—*From or by---*	Mnoda ikok—*From or by bags.*
Nom:—Pilaskw—*Paper.*	Pilaskw ol—*Papers.*
Gen:—Pilaskw'i—*Paper's.*	Pilaskw'i—*Papers'.*
Dat:—Pilaskw ok—*To paper.*	Pilaskw ikok—*To papers.*
Acc:—Pilaskw—*Paper.*	Pilaskw ol—*Papers.*
Abl:—Pilaskw ok—*From or by---*	Pilaskw ikok—*From or by---*

—ending in "n, s, o"

Singular.	Plural.
Nom:— Sen—*Stone.*	Sen al—*Stones.*
Gen:—Sen'i—*Stone's.*	Sen'i—*Stones'.*
Dat:—Sen ek—*To stone.*	Sen ikok—*To stenes.*
Acc:—Sen—*Stone.*	Sen al—*Stones.*
Abl:—Sen ek—*From or by stone.*	Sen ikok—*From or by stones.*
Nom:—Nbes—*Lake.*	Nbes al—*Lakes.*
Gen:—Nbes'i—*Lake's.*	Nbes'i—*Lakes'.*
Dat:—Nbes ek—*To lake.*	Nbes ikok—*To lakes.*
Acc:—Nbes—*Lake.*	Nbes al—*Lakes.*
Abl:—Nbes ek—*From or by---*	Nbes ikok—*From or by lakes.*
Nom:—Pikon—*String.*	Pikon al—*Strings.*
Gen:—Pikon'i—*String's.*	Pikon'i—*Strings'.*
Dat:—Pikon ek—*To string.*	Pikon ikok—*To strings.*
Acc:—Pikon—*String.*	Pikon al—*Strings.*
Abl:—Pikon ek—*From or by---*	Pikon ikok—*From or by strings.*
Nom:—Sibo—*River.*	Sibo al—*Rivers.*
Gen:—Sibo'i—*River's.*	Sibo'i—*Rivers'.*
Dat:—Sibo k—*To river.*	Sibo ikok—*To rivers.*
Acc:—Sibo—*River.*	Sibo al—*Rivers.*
Abl:—Sibo k—*From or by---*	Sibo ikok—*From or by rivers.*

THE ADJECTIVE

An adjective is a word used to qualify nouns.

Adjectives are divided into two principal classes:—

1—Strong adjectives qualify Strong Nouns.
2—Weak Adjectives qualify Weak Nouns.

Ajectives agree in number, gender and case with the nouns they qualify.

Examples:—

San8ba mlikigo—*The man is strong.*

San8ba, Strong noun, Noble gender, Nom. case, Sing. number.
Mlikigo, Strong Adj. Noble gender, Nom. case, Sing number.

San8bak Mlikigoak—*The men are strong.*

San8bak, Strong noun, Noble gender, Nom. case, Plural number.
Mlikigoak, Strong Adj. Noble gender, Nom. case, Plural number.

Kl8gan mlikigen—*The door is strong.*

Kl8gan, Weak noun, Common gender, Nom. case, Sing. number.
Mlikigen, Weak Adj., Common gender, Nom. case, Sing. number.

Kl8ganal mlikigenol—*The doors are strong.*

Kl8ganal, Weak noun, Common gender, Nom. case, 3rd person plural.
Mlikigenol, Weak adj., Common gender, Nom. case, 3rd person plu.

Aln8ba nhla masgiliji moza—*The Indian kills a big moose.*

Moza, Strong noun, Noble gender, Acc. case, 3rd person singular.
Masgiliji, Strong adj., Noble gender, Acc. case, 3rd person singular.

Phanem wlito walikkil assolkw8nal—*The woman makes good
    hats.*

Assolkw8nal, Weak noun, Com. gender, Acc. case, 3rd person plural.
Walikkil, Weak adj., Com. gender, Acc. case, 3rd person plural.

Aln8bak wlitoak walikkil abasnodaal—*The Indians make fine
    baskets.*

Abasnodaal, Weak noun, Com. gender, Acc. case, 3rd person plural.
Walikkil, Weak adj., Com. gender, Acc. case, 3rd person plural.

Wligo asses—*Good horse.*
Wligen 8wdi—*Good road.*

It would not be right to say: "Wligen asses" because wligen
is a weak adjective and asses a strong noun; nor would it be right
to say: "Wligo 8wdi" because "wligo" is a strong adjective and
"8wdi" a weak noun.

Wligoak assessak—*Good horses.*

It would not be right to say: "Wligo assessak" though both
the adjective and noun are strong but because the adjective "wligo"
is in the singular number and "assessak" in the plural.

ATTRIBUTIVE

Strong Adjectives are declined thus:—

Singular.	Plural.
Nom:—Wal igid—*Good, handsome.*	Wal igid jik—
Acc:—Wal igidji—	Wal igili ji—
Nom:—Maj igid—*Bad, ugly.*	Maj igid jik—
Acc:— Maj igidji—	Maj igili ji—
Nom:—W8b igid—*White.*	W8b igid jik—
Acc:—W8b igidji—	W8b igili ji—
Nom:—Chila id—*Peevish.*	Chila ijik—
Acc:—Chila idji—	Chila iliji—
Nom:—Kwan izid—*Long.*	Kwan izid jik—
Acc:—Kwan izid ji—	Kwan izili ji—
Nom:—Pew sess id—*Small.*	Pew sess ijik—
Acc:—Pew sess iji—	Pew sess iliji—
Nom:—Nok igid—*Soft.*	Nok igid jik—
Acc:—Nok igidji—	Nok igili ji—

PREDICATE

Strong Adjectives.

Singular:—Wligo—*He or she is good, handsome.*
Plural:—Wligoak—*They are good, handsome.*

Singular:—Majigo—*He or she is bad, ugly.*
Plural:—Majigoak—*They are bad, ugly.*

Singular:—W8bigo—*He or she is white.*
Plural:—W8bigoak—*They are white.*

Singular:—Chilao—*He or she is peevish.*
Plural:—Chilaoak—*They are peevish.*

Singular:—Kwnizo—*He or she is tall.*
Plural:—Kwnizoak—*They are tall.*

Singular:—Piwsesso—*He or she is small.*
Plural:—Piwsessoak—*They are small.*

Singular:—Nokigo—*He or she is soft.*
Plural:—Nokigoak—*They are soft.*

Singular:—Mkwigo—*He or she is red.*
Plural:—Mkwigoak—*They are red.*

ATTRIBUTIVE

Weak adjectives are declined thus:—

Singular.	Plural.
Nom:—Wlig en—*Good.*	Wlig nol—
Acc:—Walig ek—	Walig kil—
Nom:—Majig en—*Bad.*	Majig nol—
Acc:—Majig ek—	Majig kil—
Nom:—W8big en—*White.*	W8big nol—
Acc:—W8big ek—	W8big kil—
Nom:—Piw sess en—*Small.*	Piw sess nol—
Acc:—Piw sess ek—	Piw sess gil—
Nom:—Nokig en—*Soft.*	Nokig nol—
Acc:—Nokig ek—	Nokig kil—
Nom:—Nojmig en—*Weak.*	Nojmig nol—
Nojmig ek—	Nojmig kil—
Nom:—Mlikig en—*Strong.*	Mlikig nol—
Mlikig ek—	Mlikig kil—

List of Strong and Weak Adjectives.

Ada.

Strong.	Weak.
Adagigid—	Adagigek—*False.*
Askasgwigid—	Askaskwigek—*Green.*
Azawaskwigid—	Azawaskwigek—*Square.*
Kapagisid—	Kapagak—*Thick.*
Kwanakwzid—	Kwanak—*Long, tall.*
Majigid—	Majigek—*Bad.*
Makwigid—	Makwigek—*Red.*
Masalkik—	Masalkil—*Many.*
Nokigid—	Nokigek—*Soft.*
Nospigid—	Nospigek—*High.*
S8klizid—	S8glak—*Hard.*
Taakwizid—	Taakwak—*Short.*

Strong adjectives ending in "id" form their plural by adding "jik" as waligid, waligidjik. Ending in "ak" add "ik" as sazig8dak sazig8dakik.

Weak adjectives ending in "en" form their plural by adding "ol" as wligen, wligenol. Ending in "a" add "l" as s8gla, s8glal.

THE INFLECTION OF THE ADJECTIVE

The Positive expresses a quality simply, as Mlikigo—*Strong.*

The Comparative expresses a higher or lower degree of quality than the Positive; as Paami mlikigo—*Stronger,*
Nod8 mlikigo—*Less strong.*

The superlative expresses a quality in the highest degree, as
P8baami mlikigo—*Strongest,*
Paami nod8 mlikigo—*The least strong.*

The comparative and Superlative are formed by putting Paami and P8bami respectively before the Positive as,
Positive—Wligo—*Good,* Comparative—Paami wligo—*Better,* Superlative—P8bami wligo—*Best.*

The Diminution of degree is expressed by prefixing nod8 and paami nod8 to the Positive as,
Positive:—Wligo—*Good.* Comparative:—Nod8 wligo—*Less good.* Superlative:—Paami nod8 wligo—*Least good.*

ADJECTIVE PREFIXES PLUS NOUN SUFFIXES

Akw plus bi—*Bitter water, Rum.*
Alna plus hlakw—*Hard metal, Iron.*
Alni plus gamikw—*Indian wigwam.*
Al8m plus sakw—*Inside room.*
Awas plus naga—*Opposite shore.*

Chebi plus gamikw—*Separate building.*

Kchi plus tekw—*Great, Main river.*
Kaka plus sokw—*Clear sky.*
Kika plus jiwi—*Close to edge.*
Kini plus b8kka—*Very rough land.*
Koa plus tekw—*Pine river.*
Kta plus aden—*Great rock or mountain.*
Kweni plus tekw—*Long river.*

Mada plus h8ndo—*Bad spirit, devil.*
Mada plus l8kw—*Useless kettle.*
Mada plus sem—*Good for nothing animal.*
Madj plus gisgad—*Bad day.*
Mdawa plus kwam—*Cheering or May pole.*

Namas plus kik8n—*Fish field.*
Namas plus 8lo—*Fish tail.*

Pilwi plus ki—*Different land.*
Pne plus g8kw—*Falling hill.*
Pokja plus nakw—*Part of tree, stump.*
P8n plus tekw—*Rapid, falling river.*

Ska plus hla—*Raw hide.*
Ska plus kwam—*Green wood.*
Ska plus wakw—*Fresh meat.*
Ski plus bakw—*Green leaf.*
Spem plus ki—*Up land, heaven.*
Spem plus sakw—*Up room, up stairs.*
Squa plus sem—*Female beast.*

Tma plus nakw—*Part of tree trunk, stub.*

Walas plus tekw—*Shallow river.*
Wja plus kwam—*Butt end of tree.*
Wle plus gisgad—*Nice day.*
Wl8gwi plus hlas—*Evening bird.*
W8b plus apskw—*White rock.*
W8bi plus m8ni—*White money.*
Wski plus gen—*New vegetable.*

PRONOUNS

A pronoun is a word used instead of a noun and sometimes as an adjective limiting a noun.

Pronouns are divided into two principal classes:—

1—Strong Pronouns,
2—Weak Pronouns.

Each class of pronouns is subdivided into Substantive and Adjective Pronouns.

Strong Pronouns are used instead of strong Nouns.
Weak Pronouns are used instead of weak Nouns.

Substituting Strong Nouns.

Personal Pronouns.

Nia—*I.*
Niona—*We.*
Kia—*Thou or you.*
Kiow8—*You.*

Demonstrative

Agma—*He or she.*
Agm8w8—*They.*
Uwa—*This.*
Yugik—*These.*
Yanm8—*That.*
Yagik—*Those.*
Yanm8gik—*Those, more than two.*

Strong Pronouns

Substituting Strong Nouns.

Relative

Enna—*Who.*

Interogative.

Awani—*Who.*
T8nwa—*Which.*

Indefinite.

T8nitta awani—*Any body.*
Awani—*Some body.*
8nda awani—*Nobody.*
Kdak awani—*Other person.*

Substituting Weak Nouns.

Demonstrative

Iyo—*This.*
Yolil—*These.*
Iya—*That.*
Yalil—*Those.*

Weak Pronouns

Substituting Weak Nouns.

Enni—*Which.*

Interogative.

Kaguessa—*What.*
T8nyo—*Which.*

Indefinite.

T8nitta kagui—*Any thing.*
Kawi—*Something.*
8ndakagui—*Nothing.*
Kdak kagui—*Other thing.*

DEMONSTRATIVE ADJECTIVE PRONOUNS DECLINED

Third Person Singular

Nom:—Agma—*He or she.*
Gen:—Agma'iya—*His or hers.*
Dat:—Agmak—*To him or her.*
Acc:—Agma—*Him or her.*
Abl:—Agmak—*From or by---*

Third Person Plural

Agm8w8—*They.*
Agm8w8'iya—*Theirs.*
Agm8w8k—*To them.*
Agm8w8—*Them.*
Agm8w8k—*From or by them.*

PERSONAL PRONOUNS DECLINED

First Person Singular

Nom:—Nia—*I.*
Gen:—Nia'iya—*Mine.*
Dat:—Niak—*To me.*
Acc:—Nia—*Me.*
Abl:—Niak—*From or by me.*

First Person Plural

Niona—*We.*
Niona'iya—*Ours.*
Nionak—*To us.*
Niona—*Us.*
Nionak—*From or by us.*

Second Person Singular

Nom:—Kia—*Thou or you.*
Gen:—Kia'iya—*Thine.*
Dat:—Kiak—*To thee or you.*
Acc.—Kia—*You.*
Abl:—Kiak—*From or by you.*

Second Person Plural

Kiow8—*You.*
Kiow8'iya—*Yours.*
Kiow8k—*To you.*
Kiow8—*You.*
Kiow8k—*From or by you.*

PERSONAL PRONOUNS AND DEMONSTRATIVE ADJECTIVES

Ownership is also expressed by Personal Pronoun and Demonstrative Adjective prefixes used with Strong Nouns beginning with a vowel or the letter "s" viz:

Nd for my and ours; Kd for thy and your; Wd for his, her and their or simply N, K, W, if the noun begins with a consonant except "s".

Examples:—

Nd'awikhigan—*My book.*
Kd'awikhigan—*Thy book.*
Wd'awikhigan—*His or her book.*
N'wigw8m—*My wigwam.*
K'wigw8m—*Thy wigwam.*
W'wigw8m—*His or her wigwam.*

Nd'awikhiganna—*Our book.*
Kd'awikhiganw8—*Your book.*
Wd'awikhiganw8—*Their book.*
N'wigw8mna—*Our wigwam.*
K'wigw8mw8—*Your wigwam.*
W'wigw8mw2—*Their wigwam.*

The Declension of nouns and adjectives admits the nominative singular as the leading case, the others being derived from it.

The combination of the Personal Pronoun or the Demonstrative Adjective with a Strong Noun forms a compound Strong Noun which is declined as a simple Strong Noun except that the Nominative Singular must first be found.

For the Nominative Singular of Compound Strong Nouns.

The Strong Noun.

Ending in a, i, o, add "m".
Ending in ikw, gw, ai, ch, or any consonant, add "em".
Ending in skw, akw, agw, add "om".

Examples:—

San8ba—*Man.*   N'san8bam—*My man.*
Titgeli—*Owl.*   N'titgelim—*My owl.*
Pit8lo—*Lion.*   N'pit8lom—*My lion.*
Akikw—*Seal.*   Nd'akikwem—*My seal.*
K8gw—*Porcupine.*   N'gogwem—*My porcupine.*
Chibai—*Ghost.*   N'chibaiem—*My ghost.*
Awanoch—*French.*   Nd'awanochem—*My Frenchman.*
Moz—*Moose.*   N'mozem—*My moose.*

For the Nominative Singular of Compound Strong Nouns.

To the Strong Noun,

Ending in agw, akw, and skw, add "om".

Exemples:—

Namagw—*Salmon trout.*   N'namagw om—*My salmon trout.*
Kaakw—*Gull.*   N'kaakw om—*My gull.*
Agaskw—*Ground hog.*   Nd'agasgw om—*My ground hog.*

VERBS

Verbs are divided into three classes:—

1—Strong. 2—Weak. 3—Neuter.

Strong and Weak verbs are transitive and each requires a noun of like force for its object, in the accusative case.

Neuter is intransitive verb.

It is evident that the Indian can express his thoughts and actions as clearly and to the point, as the White man, because his verbs are simple, short and full of meaning. He uses only three tenses; Present, Past and Future, but, in case he wanted to express the Perfect of these, he can do so by simply putting "Kizi" before the first two and transferring the "Ji" of the Future Tense to "Kizi" thus "Kiziji".

I—STRONG VERB

Waji Mow8mek—*To eat.*

INDICATIVE MOOD

PRESENT TENSE

Singular.	Plural.
N'mow8—*I eat.*	N'mow8nna—*We eat.*
K'mow8—*Thou eatest.*	K'mow8w8—*You eat.*
W'mow8 *He or she eats.*	W'mow8w8—*They eat.*

PRESENT PERFECT

Kizi N'mow8—*I have eaten.*   Kizi N'mow8nna—*We have eaten*

PAST TENSE

N'mow8p—*I ate.*	N'mow8nop—*We ate.*
K'mow8p—*Thou atest.*	K'mow8w8p—*You ate.*
W'mow8p—*He ate.*	W'mow8w8p—*They ate.*

PAST PERFECT

Kizi n'mow8p—*I had eaten.*   Kizi n'mow8nnop—*We had eaten*

FUTURE TENSE

N'mow8ji—*I will eat.*	N'mow8nnaji—*We will eat.*
K'mow8ji—*Thou shalt eat.*	K'mow8w8ji—*You shall eat.*
W'mow8ji—*He shall eat.*	W'mow8w8ji—*They shall eat.*

FUTURE PERFECT

Kiziji N'mow8—*I will have eaten*   Kiziji N'mow8nna—*We will have eaten*

SUBJUNCTIVE MOOD

PRESENT TENSE

Chaga N'mow8n—*If I eat.*	Chaga N'mow8nana—*If we eat.*
Chaga K'mow8n—*If thou eat.*	Chaga K'mow8n8—*If you eat.*
Chaga W'mow8n—*If he eat.*	Chaga W'mow8n8—*If they eat.*

IMPERATIVE MOOD

PRESENT TENSE

Mowakia—*Eat thou.*   Mowok kiow8—*Eat you.*

INFINITIVE MOOD	*PARTICIPLE*
Waji mow8mek—*To eat.*	Mow8mek—*Eating.*

II—WEAK VERB

Waji Mij8zik—*To eat.*

INDICATIVE MOOD
PRESENT TENSE

Singular	Plural
N'miji—*I eat.*	N'mijibna—*We eat.*
K'miji—*Thou eatst.*	K'mijiba—*You eat.*
W'mijo—*He eats.*	W'mijoak—*They eat.*

PRESENT PERFECT TENSE

Kizi N'miji—*I have eaten.*	Kizi N'mijibna—*We have eaten.*

PAST TENSE

N'mijib—*I ate.*	N'mijibnop—*We ate.*
K'mijib—*Thou atest.*	K'mijib8p—*You ate.*
W'mijob—*He ate.*	W'mijobanik—*They ate.*

PAST PERFECT TENSE

Kizi N'mijib—*I had eaten.*	Kizi N'mijibnop—*We had eaten.*

FUTURE TENSE

N'mijiji—*I will eat.*	N'mijibnaji—*We will eat.*
K'mijiji—*Thou shalt eat.*	K'mijibaji—*You will eat.*
W'mijoji—*He shall eat.*	W'mijoakji—*They will eat.*

FUTURE PERFECT TENSE

Kiziji N'miji—*I will have eaten.*	Kiziji N'midsibna—*We will have eaten.*

SUBJUNCTIVE MOOD

PRESENT TENSE

Chaga N'mijin—*If I eat.*	Chaga N'mijinana—*If we eat.*
Chaga K'mijin—*If thou eat.*	Chaga K'mijin8.—*If you eat.*
Chaga W'mijin—*If he eat.*	Chaga N'mijin8—*If they eat.*

IMPERATIVE MOOD
PRESENT TENSE

Miji kia—*Eat thou.*	Mijikw kiow8—*Eat you.*

INFINITIVE MOOD
PRESENT TENSE

Waji Mij8zik—*To eat.*

PARTICIPLE
PRESENT
Mij8zik—*Eating.*

III—NEUTER OR INTRANSITIVE VERB
Waji Midsimek—*To eat.*

INDICATIVE MOOD
PRESENT TENSE

N'midsi—*I eat.*	N'midsibna—*We eat.*
K'midsi—*Thou eatst.*	K'midsiba—*You eat.*
W'midso—*He eats.*	W'midsoak—*They eat.*

PRESENT PERFECT TENSE

Singular	Plural
Kizi N'midsi—*I have eaten.*	Kizi N'midsibna—*We have eaten.*

PAST TENSE

N'midsib—*I ate.*	N'midsibnop—*We ate.*
K'midsib—*Thou atest.*	K'midsib8b—*You ate.*
W'midsop—*He ate.*	W'midsobanik—*He ate.*

PAST PERFECT TENSE

Kizi N'midsib—*I had eaten.*	Kizi N'midsibnop—*We had eaten.*

FUTURE TENSE

N'midsiji—*I will eat.*	N'midsibnaji—*We shall eat.*
K'midsiji—*Thou shalt eat.*	K'midsibaji—*You shall eat.*
W'midsoji—*He shall eat.*	W'midsoakji—*They shall eat.*

FUTURE PERFECT TENSE

Kiziji N'midsi—*I will have eaten.*	Kiziji N'midsibna—*We will have eaten.*

SUBJUNCTIVE MOOD
PRESENT TENSE

Singular	Plural
Chaga N'midsin—*If I eat.*	Chaga N'midsinana—*If we eat.*

IMPERATIVE MOOD
PRESENT TENSE

Midsi kia—*Eat thou.*	Minsikw kiow8—*Eat you.*

INFINITIVE MOOD
PRESENT TENSE

Waji Midsimek—*To eat.*

VERBS

STRONG	WEAK
Waji Agakim8mek	Waji Agakid8zik—*To Teach.*
" Awikhamaw8mek	" Awikh8zik—*To Write.*
" Chigitaw8mek	" Chigit8zik—*To Let.*
" Chigitwa8mek	" Chigitwa8zik—*To Shave.*
" Katam8mek	
" Kazalm8mek	" Kazald8zik—*To Love.*
" Kik8m8mek	" Kik8d8zik—*To Curse.*
" Kisp8wl8mek	" Kisp8wd8zik—*To Scare.*
" Kwatalm8mek	" Kwatad8zik—*To Mistrust.*
" Kwilawa8mek	" Kwilawat8zik—*To Search.*
" Kwzial8mek	" Kwziad8zik—*To Swallow.*
" Maskaw8mek	" Mask8zik—*To Find.*
" Mil8mek	" Mild8zik—*To Give.*
" Mow8mek	" Mij8zik—*To Eat.*
" Mozmaw8mek	" Mozm8zik—*Hair cut.*
" Nadmih8mek	" —*To Lend.*
" Nadodmaw8mek	" —*To Ask.*
" Nadom8mek	" Nadod8zik—*To Miss.*
" Nanawalm8mek	" Nanawald8zik—*To Keep.*
" Nbakadaw8mek	" —*To Cheat.*
" Ngal8mek	" Ngad8zik—*To Leave.*
" Nosokaw8mek	" Nosok8zik—*To Follow.*
" Odakaw8mek	" Odak8zik—*To Visit.*

The Infinitive Mood, Present Tense of all Strong and Neuter Verbs end in "mek" and the Weak Verbs in "zik".

LIST OF NEUTER OR INTRANSITIVE VERBS

Waji Abimek—*To Sit.*
   " Adbiguahl8mek—*To Roll.*
   " Azidguakag8bimek—*To Kneel.*

   " Kagalnakwimek—*To Cling.*
   " Kawimek—*To Sleep.*
   " Kdahl8mek—*To Sink.*
   " Kin8baimek—*To Dare.*

Waji Ligdahimek—*To Jump.*
    "   L8bagipozimek—*To Swing.*

    "   Machinamek—*To Die.*
    "   Madw8zimek—*To Murmur.*
    "   Majdonkamek—*To Blasphems.*

    "   Nakwh8mimek—*To Sneeze.*
    "   Nguediguawimek—*To Wink.*
    "   Nguit8kwzimek—*To soliloquize.*

    "   8dokazlmek—*To Converse.*
    "   8mikimek—*To Rise.*

    "   Polwamek—*To Flee.*
    "   Pmeg8mek—*To Dance.*
    "   Pmigwzimek—*To Crawl.*

    "   Tbidah8zimek—*To Think.*

ADVERBS

An adverb is a word which modifies a verb, adjective or another adverb.

A list af adverbes

Alwa—*Almost.*

Chiga—*When.*

Kdem8giwi—*Poorly.*
Kskamiwi—*Across.*
Kwaskwai—*Enough.*

M8manni—*Slowly.*

Natamiwi—*First.*
Ngemiwi—*Easily.*
Nidali—*There.*
Nikw8bi—*Now.*
Nilliwi—*Thus.*

N8wadoga—*Far.*

Paliwi—*Elsewhere.*
Pita—*Very.*

Sipkiwi—*Late.*
S8waiwi—*Often.*

Ta8lawini—*Thus.*
T8ndaka—*Where.*

Wlidbiwi—*Well.*
Wz8mi—*Too much.*

Yudali—*Here.*

ADVERB PREFIX PLUS VERBAL ROOT

Chibagi plus t8gwzimek—*Speaking loudly.*
Chit8z plus samek— *Walking farther.*

K8do plus samek—*Walking privily.*

Mannin plus t8zik—*Singing slowly.*
Manno plus samek—*Walking slowly.*
Msal plus higamek—*Shooting many arrows.*

Nopas plus samek—*Walking far away.*

Piswa plus lokamek—*Working for nothing.*
Pedgo plus samek—*Walking back.*

Saag8w plus zimek— *Living poorly.*
S8gnauw8w plus zimek—*Living peaceably.*

Tagas8w plus zimek—*Living sparingly.*
Tagassi plus pimek—*Eating sparingly.*

Wiwhiz8 plus samek—*Walking hastily.*
Wiwni plus taigamek—*Knocking around.*
Wlidbi plus Klozimek—*Speaking correctly.*

THE PRINCIPAL PREPOSITIONS

Abichiwi—*Against.*
Ajichiwi—*Beside.*

Kassiwi—*With.*
Kikajiwi—*Close by.*
Kottliwi—*Among.*
Kskamiwi—*Across.*
Kwahliwi—*Near.*
Kwelbiwi—*Behind.*

Li—*To.*

Naguiwi—*Under.*
Nik8niwi—*Before.*

Oji—*From.*

P8zijiwi—*Over.*

Spemek—*Up.*
S8biwi—*Throuhg.*

Tali—*At.*
Tapsiwi—*Down.*

THE PRINCIPAL CONJUNCTIONS

Ala—*Or.*
Achigaba—*Hawever.*
Askwa—*Yet.*

Kagna—*Lest.*
Kanwa—*But.*
Kwana—*Whilst.*

Lli—*Until.*

Minaguiba—*Though.*

Ninawa—*Therefore.*
Nioji—*Then.*
Niwadtak—*Hence.*

Ojikawi—*Why.*

8ndaki—*Than.*

Ta—*And.*
Ta8lawi—*As.*

Wz8mi—*Because.*

INTERJECTIONS

An Interjection is an exclamation expressing some sudden emotion of the mind but has no grammatical relation with other words in a sentence: as,

Saagin8kw! N'wigw8m chgata.
Alas! my wigwam is on fire.

Kam8jigaki! Saagad!
Oh! It is too bad.

Niayaga!
Oh! It was destined to end so!

N8nsojin8guat!
Oh! What a misfortune.

Nidoba kn8ji waw8dokawel ali k'dadan machinad!
    Ah! N'dadan machina O kia wijokamessina.
My friend I come to inform you, that your father is dead. ...
    Ah! my father is dead O you! Do help us.

Ahaa! Ngemiskzak8gaba Enni Ayu!
    Aha! You are beaten Ayu! Ayu!

Wha! Wha! kedm8gi pagah8 kawiba kia kisitowan.
    Wha! Wha! poor devil what can you do!

PART III

THE MEANING OF INDIAN NAMES
OF RIVERS, LAKES, ETC.

THE MEANING OF INDIAN NAMES
OF RIVERS, LAKES, ETC.

— A —

AQWANUS or GOYNISH, a river running into the north shore of the Gulf of St. Lawrence, east of the Mingan Island.

Agwanus means Conoe Birch Bark peeled, out of season i. e. after July when there is no more sap. The sapwood then becomes just like glue holding fast the wood and bark together. The bark is very hard to peel, it must sometimes be heated with a burning piece of birch bark and then skinned. In order to scrape off the sapwood, sticking to the bark, it must be steamed with boiling water, if not removed before the canoe is made, the water would sooner or later permeate the substance causing thereby an additional weight to the canoe and making it hard to manage.

"Igua" means one strip of birch bark to make one canoe, hence "Agwanus-igua" means one strip of this kind of bark to make one canoe.

AROOSTOOK, an important tributary of the St. John, rises in the State of Maine and following a general N. E. course, falls into the St. John a little above Tobique, N. B.

Aroostook from Wlastekw.

Prefix "Wlas" means bright, "tekw" means river.

Aroostook, Aroosaguntook and Alsiguntook are designations of the same river Aroostook.

— B —

BASKAHEGAN RIVER, ME. This river rises in a large lake of the same name, in the County of Washington, near the line of New Brunswick.

Baskahegan means an old and unfrequented way.

— C —

COATICOOK RIVER, rises in the State of Vermont and entering the County of Compton, Que., runs N. E. into the St. Francis.

Coaticook from Koatekwog meaning to the Pine River.

"Koa" means Pine,   Suffix "tekw" means river.

Declined:

> Nom:—Koatekw—*The Pine River.*
> Gen:—Koatekw'i—*Of the Pine River.*
> Dat:—Koatekw og—*To the Pine River.*
>
> See Story IV.

COUCOUCACHE, a river and lake of Quebec, between the Rivers Flammand and Vermillon which run E. into the St. Maurice, above Bostonnais river.

(Coucoucache) from Kokokhas meanig an owl.   See Story I.

CONNECTICUT RIVER has its source in New Hampshire and the Mountainous tracts of Quebec Province.

Connecticut from Kwnitekw meaning long river.

Prefix "Kwni" means long, Suffix "tekw" means river.

> See Story V.

CUSHNOE was the name given to Augusta Me. by the Indians.

Cushoe from Kassinoak meaning living together. It was so callad because the Whites got to be so many that they and the Indians were apparently living together.

CHESUNCOOK LAKE, ME. In the County of Pescataquis, is a large sheet of water through which the Penobsoot river passes.

Chesuncook from Kchisen'itekw meaning to the big stones lake.

> Nom. Plural:—Kchisenal—*The big stones lake.*
> Gen.   "   Kchisen'i—*Of the big stones lake.*
> Dat.   "   Kchisen'ikok—*To the big stones lake.*

COBSCOOK BAY, ME. A large bay, the recipient of a number of large ponds on the S. W. side of Eastport, in Passamaquody Bay.

Cobscook from Apskw ok meaning tide water falling bay.

CHIPQUEDOPSKOOK is the main outlet of Eagle Lake, Me.

Chipquedopskook from Kchi pkwe d apskw ok meaning to the great split rock.

Prefix "Kchi" means great, "pkwe" means slit, "d" for eu phony, "apskw" means rock, "ok" final of Dative case, to or at.

Apskw declined:

Nom:—Apskw—*The rock.*
Gen:—Apskw'i—*Of the rock.*
Dat:—Apskw ok—*To or at the rock.*

COHASET, MASS., Norfolk Co. A town on Massachusetts Bay noted for its rocky coast and numerous shipwrecks.

Cohaset from Koasek meaning to the small pine tree or grove of pine trees.

Declined.

Singular Nom:—Koas—*The small pine tree.*
   "   Gen:—Koas'i—*Of the small pine tree.*
   "   Dat:—Koasek—*To the small pine tree .*

CONAQUETOGUE pond (salt water) at Charlestown, Washington Co. R. I.

Conaquetogue from Kwnaquatekw meaning a long pond.

Prefix "Kwna" or "Kwnaqua" means long, Suffix "tekw" means river or pond.

CASCO BAY, ME.

Casco from Kasko meaning Crane.   This is one of the finest bays on the American Coast.

CHARLOTTE, VT. This is a pleasant town, in Chittenden Co., on Lake Champlain and opposite to Essex, N. Y. In Essex, about three miles across the lake is Split Rock, a great natural curiosity. Our fathers and grand fathers believed that this Rock represented the god and goddess of the Wind and they never went by without leaving either a pipe or tobacco at the foot of it and begging for a favorable wind or no wind.

CONTOOCOOK RIVER, N. H.

Contoocook from Nik8ntekw ok.

Prefix "Nik8n" means first of head branch, Suffix "tekw" means river, "ok" means to or from.

—E—

ETCHEMIN, a river of Quebec, rises in a lake of the same name in the County of Dorchester and falls into the St. Lawrence, a short distance above Levis. Length about fifty miles. It is also called the River Bruyante from its roaring, being heard in Quebec City before a southeasterly storm.

Etchemin from atman meaning gut string.   See Story VI.

—H—

HOUSATONICK RIVER. The sources of this river are in the towns of Lanesborough and Windsor, Birkshire Co., Mass. It meets the tide water at Derby, 14 miles above its entrance into Long Island Sound.

Housatonick from Awass'adenik meaning over the mountain.

Prefix "Awassa" means Over, Suffix "Aden" means Mountain. The particle "ik" means to or at.

—K—

KENNEBUNK PORT, ME., York Co. This town is situated on the N. E. side of the Kenebunk River.

Kenebunk from Kini b8ka meaning very rough ground.

Prefix "Kinni" means very, Suffix "b8ka" means rough ground.

KATAHDIN MOUNTAIN, ME. This celebrated mountain, the greatest elevation in the state lies between the Eastern and Western branches of Penobscot river, in the County of Piscataquis.

Katahdin from Ktaaden.

Prefix "Kta" means great, grand, lofty, Suffix "Aden" means mountain.

KENOGAMI, a beautiful lake on the left of the Chicoutimi river, Que.

Kenogami means Long lake.

Prefix "Keno" means long, Suffix "gami" means lake.

KENOGAMISHISH, a small lake separated from Kenogami by a ridge about one and one half miles long by half a mile wide.

Kenogamishish is a diminutive of Kenogami, a small Kenogami or comparitively large lake. See Kenogami.

KENDUSKIAG STREAM, ME. This stream rises in Dexter and Garland. It falls into the Penobscot river at the centre of the city of Bangor.

Kenduskiag from Kinibeskiag meaning The Indians living near a real stream or lake.

— M —

MEMPHREMAGOG LAKE. This lake is about 30 miles in length, and two or three miles in width. About seven miles of it lies in the County of Orleans, the residue in Canada.

Memphremagog from Mam hlow bagw og meaning To the very extensive lake.

Prefix "Mamhlow" means much, Suffix "bagw" means lake or pond.

Mamhlowbagw means lake extending much,

Mamhlowbagwog means To the lake extending much.

Declined:

Nom:—Mamhlowbagw—*The lake extending much.*

Gen:—Mamhlowbagw'i—*Of the lake extending much.*

Dat:—Mamhlowbagw og—*To the lake extending much.*

Examples:—

Mamhlow ipo—*He eats much.*

Mamhlow esmo—*He drinks much.*

Mamhlow aka—*He hits hard.*

MASKANONGI-WAGAMING, a lake of Ontario about seven miles wide. It forms one of the sources of the Sturgeon river which empties into the N. side of Lake Nipissing.

Maskanongi-Wagaming from Maskwenoza'agamak meaning Lake full of Maskinonge or Pike.

MASSAWIPPI, a lake in the township of Hatley, County of Stanstead, Que. This lake has its outlet in the River St. Francis by the Massawippi River.

Massawippi from Massawip'i meaning of great depth.

Massa means great, Wip'i means the central part, as—*the pith of a tree.*

MATAGAMASHING, a lake in Ontario.

Mattagamsing or Matt8gamasek meaning the ontlet of the lake.

MADAWASKA RIVER, rises in Lake Temiscoata and running S. falls into the river St. John, at Edmondston, N. B.

Madawaska from Mada w aska.

Mada means useless, good for nothing; w for euphony; Aska means grasey.

Madawaska means Grass good for nothing to the main.

MATAKEESET or Duxbury, Mass, Plymouth Co. This town lies on Massachusetts Bay in Plymouth Harbor.

Matakeeset from Matagizit meaning Reckoning up being done.

Adv. prefix "Mata" means All, everything,
Verb "Agizit" means Reckoning or counting.

MASHENTUCK in Killingly, Conn. Windham Co.

Mashentuck from Maz8ntekw meaning Wild hemp pond, brook or river.

Maz8n means Wild hemp; Suffix "tekw" means pond.

MATAPAN, now Dorchester Mass. Norfolk Co. This ancient town lies on Dorchester Bay, in Boston harbor, five miles south of Boston.

Matapan from Mad8ban meaning landing place.

MASSACSICK, now Long Meadow, Mass. Hampden Co.

Massacsick from Massaksek meaning moderately large piece.

Prefix "Massa" means large; Suffix "Ksek" means diminished size.

MATTABESETT, now Middletown, Conn. Chief town of Middlesex County. It is divided into four societies or parishes.

Mattabesett from Mattabesek meaning the farthest or last part of the town.

MANITOBA, a lake immediately S. W. of Lake Winnipeg with which it is connected by the Dauphin River.

Manitoba means bad water,

Manito means bad spirit.

Suffix "ba" means water.

Examples:—

Psan ba means *full of water*
Nod8 ba means *not quite full of water.*
Tagas ba means *very little water in it.*
P8zid ba means *It is more than full of water.*

MASKACHUG RIVER is in East Greenwich R. I. Kent Co.

Maskachug from Maskajagw meaning Toad marsh river.

Maska means toad; Suffix "jagw" means marsh or pool.

MANITOU-NAMAIG, a river N. of Lake Superior, enters Kenogami river six miles from the outlet of Long Lake.

Manitou-Namaig from Monito-Namagw meaning Bad salmon trout.

MANITOWICK, a lake of the district of Algoma, Ont. Forms one of the sousces of the Michipicoten River which enters into Lake Superior.

Manitowick means Like Monito or the devil.

MASKINONGE, a lake in the township of Brandon, County of Berthier, Que., about nine miles in circumference. It is well stocked with fish.

Maskinonge from Maskwenoza meaning Great or big pike.

Prefix "Mas" means great, Radical "Kwenoza" means pike.

MATTAWAMKEAG RIVER, ME. This is one of the most important tributaries of the Penobscot.

Mattawamkeag from Mattawamkiag meaning The Indians of the farthest or last settlement.

Prefix "Matta" means the farthest or last, Suffix "wan for wigwam or settlement, "ki" means land, final "ak" means the inhabitants of that land.

MOLECHUNKAMUNK LAKE, ME. This is one of a number of large lakes extending northwest from Umbagog lake and which empty through this lake, into the Androscoggin.

Molechunkamunk from Mol8jagamak meaning

Prefix 'Mol8" means deep, Suffix "jag" means soft, as of clay or sand, "gamak" means lake.

MOLUMKUS RIVER, ME., a large tributary of the Mattawamkeag from the north. It unites with that river about eight miles above its mouth.

Mol8mkus means Deap and rocky.

MASSABESICK POND, N. H. Rockingham Co. Massabesick pond is the largest body of fresh water in the county.

Massabesick from Mass'nbesek meaning

Prefix "Massa"means Large, big, great; Radical "nbes" means pond or lake.

Nbes declined:

Nom:—Nbes—*The pond or lake.*
Gen:—Nbes'i—*Of the pond.*
Dat:—Nbesek—*To the pond.*

Massa'nbesek—*To the great pond.*

MENAN ISLAND. Grand Menan lies off the mouth of St. Croix River. Iittle Menan in Washington County, Me., lies off the harbors of Goldsborough and Steuben.

Menan from Mnahan meaning Island.

Mnahanol means islands,
Kchi mnahan means Grand island,
Mnahanis means Small island.

MILWAUKEE is the capital of Milwaukee County, Wisconsin, and is the largest city in the state. It is situated on the West shore of Lake Michigan.

Milwaukee from Milwaikki meaning The land rendering much.

Verb "Milwaik" means gives or returns, Suffix "ki" means land

MISSISSIPI, The largest river of North america is with its tributaries wholly within the boundaries of the United States.

Mississipi from Missi sipi meaning The great river.

Prefix "Missi" means great, Radical "sibo sibi or sipi" means river.

MATACHEESET INDIANS.

Matacheeset from Methodist.

The Pilgrim Fathers borrowed some corn from Methodist Indians in 1620.

MASHAPAUG now called Alexander's Lake. This beautiful sheet of water, of about a mile in length and half a mile in breadth lies in the town of Killingly, Conn.

Mashapaugfrom Massabakw meaning big pond or lake.

Adjective prefix "Massa" means big, Noun suffix "bakw" means pond or lake.

MOUSUM RIVER, ME. This river passes through York County and meets the   at Kennebunk.

Mousum from N'mosem meaning my Moose-river.

N' stands for my, Mos means moose.

The possession is expressed thus:

> N'mosem—*My moose.*
> K'mosem—*Thy moose.*
> W'mosma—*His or her moose.*

MISSISQUE RIVER, VT. This crooked river is about 75 miles in length. It rises in Orleans County and passes N. into Canada about five miles; it then returns to the state and falls into Missisque Bay, at Highgate.

Missisque from Massipsqui meaning flint.

MOS WETUSET, a few miles from Old Boston.

Mos wetuset from Mos wajosek meaning To the Moose small mountain.

Wajos declined:

> Nom:—Wajos—*Small mountain.*
> Gen:—Wajos'i—*Of the small mountain.*
> Dat:—Wajosek—*To the small mountain.*

MONADNOCK MOUNTAIN, N. H. Usually called the Grand Monadnock is situated in the towns of Jaffrey and Dublin in Cheshire County about 22 miles E. from Connecticut river and 10 miles N. of the Southern boundery of this state.

Monadnock from Mnona'denak meaning To the bare smooth mountain.

Declined:

> Nom:—Mnona'dena—*The bare, smooth mountain.*
> Gen:—Mnona'dena'i—*Of the smooth mountain.*
> Dat:—Mnona'denak—*To the smooth mountain.*

MERREMACK RIVER, N. H. One of the principal rivers of New England.

Merrimack from Mol8demak meaning deep water or deep river

Prefix "Mol8" means deep, Suffix "demak" means water.

The name of this river was at one time written Mannomake. From time immemorial, the letter "R" "r" has been superseded by the letter "L" "l" of the Abenaki alphabet.

MEGANTIC LAKE, Que., about 40 miles S. E. of Sherbrooke, abounding with lake trout and bass. Length 16 miles, average breadth 2 miles.

Megantic from Namaskontik meaning To the fish field.

Declined.

> Nom:—Namaskonki—*The fish field.*
> Gen:—Namaskonki'i—*Of the fish field.*
> Namaskonkik—*To the fish field.*

MEGUNTICOOK RIVER AND POND. This river rises in a pond of the same name in Lincolnville, Waldo Co., Me.

Megunticook from Wnigantekwog meaning To the portage river.

Wnigan means portage, Suffix "tekw" means river.

Declined:

Nom:—Wnigantekw—*The Portage River.*
Gen:—Wnigantekw'i—*Of the Portage River.*
Dat:—Wnigantekw og—*To the Portage River.*

MASSACHUSETTS. This ancient commonwealth, the mother of New England Colonies, of free states, and of American liberty, was first permanently settled by Europeans, at Plymouth, on the 22nd of December 1620.

Massachusetts from Massa josek meaning To the great mountain.

Prefix "Massa" means great, Suffix "Jos" means mountain.

Declined:

Nom:—Massajos—*The great mountain.*
Gen:—Massajos'i—*Of the great mountain.*
Dat:—Massajos'ik—*To the great mountain.*

Examples:—

Mass'8gamak—*Great lake.*
Mass'apskak—*Great rock.*
Mass'ipskoik—*Great flint stone.*

The Abenakis did occasionally go to Saddle Mountain, the highest of Massachusetts' Mountains.

MOHIGAN from Moingan meaning Wolf.

The Mohigans were called "Wolves" because they were as rapacious as these beasts.

MICHILIMAKINAC from Msalimachinak meaning Many died or killed.

—N—

NORRIDGEWOCK, ME. Chief town of Somerset County. This town is situated on both sides of Kennebec river, 28 miles N. from Augusta. This town was formerly the site of the celebrated tribe of Norridgewock Indians.

Norridgewock from Mol8joak meaning the river flowing deeply or the deep river.

Adverb prefix "Mol8" means deeply, Verb suffix "joak" means flowing.

Norridgewock was the name given by the English to the Abenaki settlement, at the foot of Norridgewock Falls, but the same site was previously called by the French Missionaries "Nurantsuak" after Mol8joak. Owing to the fact that Kenebec River is the outlet of Moose Head Lake and that it receives two important tributaries viz. Dead and Sandy rivers above Norridgewock, it is no wonder that this river was called by the Indians Kinnebak and Mol8joak.

NASHABAH or Littleton, Mass. Middlesex Co. It is 27 miles from Boston.

Nashabah from Massaba meaning much water, as when vessels or containers are nearly full.

Prefix "Massa" means great or much, Suffix "ba" means quantity of liquld.

NATTICOTT, now Litchfield, N. H. Hillsborough Co. This town was originally known by the Indian name of Natticott and by the English one of Brenton's Farm.

Natticott from Notkikad meaning farmer.

NAMASKET, now Middleborough, Mass. Plymouth Co.

Namasket from Namaski meaning Fishing place.

Namas means fish, ki means land or place.

NARRAGUAGUS RIVER AND BAY, ME. Washington Co. The river rises in several ponds and falls into a bay of the same name.

Narraguagus from Nallaguagus meaning irregular.

NAHANT, Mass. This celebrated watering place is a part of the beautiful town of Lynn. It is a peninsula, jutting out about five miles into Massachusetts bay and forms Lynn bay on the south.

Nahant means Point.

NAUGATUCK RIVER. This rises in the northern part of Litchfield County and falls into the Housatonick at Derby.

Naugatuck from Nokka tekw meaning soft ground river.

NASSAWAGG, now Lancastter, Mass. Worcester Co. This is the oldest town of the County.

Nassawagg from Nissawak meaning At or to Nashua.

NASHUA RIVER. A beautiful stream on the south part of Hillsborough County. N. H., has its source in Worcester County, Mass. It is formed of two branches called the north and south branches.

Nashua from Niswa meaning two, hence its name Nashua.

NEWICHWANNOCK RIVER, N. H. Newichwannock or Salmon Fall river is the principal branch of the Piscatagua.

Newichwannock from N8wijoanek meaning To the long rapids and falls.

Adverb prefix "N8wi" means long distance, Participle suffix "Joan" means flowing.

N8wijoan declined:

Nom:—N8wijoan—*The long rapids.*
Gen:—N8wijoan'i—*Of the long rapids.*
Dat:—N8wijoanek—*To the long rapids.*

NARRAGANSET. Indians' territory extended about 30 or 40 miles from the Sekunk River and Narraganset Bay including Rhode Island and other islands in the bay (Drake's Indians of North America).

Narraganset from Nalwagosat meaning He goes or lands anywhere.

The Narragansets were powerful and fearless. They respected not the possessions of other Indians.

NULHEGAN RIVER, VT. This river rises by several branches in the highlands, at the north part of Essex County. This, the Abenaki Indian route between Canada and Connectucut, was also used in trapping with a device called Kulhegan, hence the name Nulhegan.

— O —

OLAMMON, ME. now Greenbush, Me. Olammon stream, one of the most beautiful tributaries of the Penobscot.

Olammon from Olamman meaning Vermillon, Sandbar.

OMPOMPONOOSUC RIVER, VT. This river rises near the centre of the County of Orange and falls into Connecticut river at Norwich.

Ompomponoosuc from Ompomponuzek meaning Mush, water queechy.

— P —

MOUNT PISGAH, Litchfield Co.

Pisgah from Pisga meaning dark. Mount Pisgah is in the rear of Colebrook and looks dark.

PASSUMPSICK RIVER, VT. This river rises in Caledonia and on the south border of Essex counties. It passes south about 35 miles and falls into the Connecticut.

Passumpsick from Passomqassik meaning Fine tumid land,

Prefix "Passom" means puffy, Suffix "Kassik" means fine sand.

PISCATAGUA RIVER, N. H. The only large river whose entire course is in the New Hampshire is formed by the junction of several small streams in a wide and deep bed.

Piscataqua from Pesgatakwa meaning The water looks dark.

Pesgata means It is dark, Suffix "akwa" means Trees or forest.

PISCATAQUIS RIVER, ME. The head waters of this river are found in the highlands which separate the waters of Penobscot and Kenebec rivers. Its length is about 65 miles.

Piscataquis from Pesgatakwis meaning a small Pesgataqua.

PISCATAQUOG RIVER, N. H., is formed of two principal branches, one from Francestown, the other from Kenniker and Deering.

Piscataquog from Pesgatawog meaning To Pesgataqua (which see).

PEMIGEWASET RIVER, N. H. This stream and Winnepis-sogee constitute the Merremack.

Pemigewaset from Pamijoussek meaning The river having its course through here.

PENABSKOK, meaning Rock inclined downwards.

PUSHAK LAKE, ME. This lake lies in the towns of Orono, Dutton and Kirkland, Penobscot Co. It empties into Dead stream.

Pushaw lak from Passa bakw meaning Lake water rising.

Prefix "Passa" means rising, Suffix "Bakw" means Pond or lake.

PASSADUMKEAG, ME. Penobscot Co. This flourishing village lies at the junction of Passadumkeag river with the Penobscot.

Passadumkeag from Passadumkiak.

Passa means rising, Dumki means land under water.

Passadumki means land under water rising, Sandbar.

Passadumkiak means The Indians living at or near that place.

PEJEPSCO, now Danville, Me., Cumberland Co.

Pejepsco means bad rock.

PATUKET or Plymouth, Mass., lies 35 miles from Boston. Plymouth was the first town built in New England by civilized man.

Patuket from Padaksit meaning Whocame sailing.

POCUMTUCK or Deerfield River, Franklin Co. Mass. This beautiful and important Indian stream joins the Connecticut between Freenfiield and Deerfield.

Pocumtuck from Pokw8mtekw meaning Very narrow river.

PAQUOIG or Athel, Mass, This pleasant place lies 60 miles from Boston.

Paquoig from Pakwaik, place for arrows.

PENOBSCOT RIVER AND BAY, ME. This large and important river has many branches and receives many tributaries. Below the union of the eastern and western branches, the Piscataquis and Matawamkeag are the largest tributaries. From the junction of the two branches to tide water at Bangor is about 76 miles.

Penobscot from Penabskok meaning Rock inclined downwards.

— Q —

QUINEBAUG RIVER. This beautiful stream rises in Mashapaug pond in Union, Conn.

Quinebaug from Kwni bakw meaning Long stream.

Prefix "Kwni" means long, Suffix "Bawk" means pond or stream.

QUINEPIAC RIVER, Conn. This river rises in Bristol and Farmington and falls into Long Island Sound at New Haven.

Quinepiac from Kwni biak meaning paddling a long distance.

Prefix "Kwni" means long, Suffix "biak" means paddling.

QUANSHIPAUG, now Mendon, Worcester Co. Mass. This pleasant town lies 32 miles S. W. from Boston.

Quanshipaug from Kwanipok meaning all winter.

Prefix "Kwani" means So long as it is, Suffix "pok" means winter.

QUEBEC CITY, Capital of Quebec Province, is situated on the left bank of the River St. Lawrence, 180 miles N. E. of Montreal.

Quebec from Nkebak meaning Under water. We learn by tradition that the lower town of Quebec was now and then partly submerged and remained under water for some time and that was when the Abenaki Indians used to come down there from Kenebec.

— S —

SHAWINIGAN, a post village in St. Maurice County, Que., on the river St. Maurice, 23 miles from Three Rivers. The stupendous Falls of the Shawinigan, 150 feet high and second only to Niagara, are in the vicinity.

Shawinigan from Wazwanigan meaning Turning or winding portage.

Prefix "Wazwa" means turning, Suffix "nigan" means portage.

SEBAGO LAKE, ME. Cumberland Co. This is a beautiful sheet of water, about 12 miles in length and of various breadths.

Sebago from Segago meaning It vomits or flushes out through the outlet.

SACO RIVER is one of the largest in New England. The whole length of Saco river is estimated to be 160 miles, running in its general course S. S.E.

Saco from Soko meaning Towards the South.

SEBASTICOOK RIVER, ME. This river rises in Sangerville, Dover and Dexter on the border of Penebscot and Piscataquis counties.

Sebasticook from Sigbastekwog meaning To the empty river.

SKOOTUM LAKE, ME. A sheet of water of considerable size, the outlet of which passes through Kilmarnock.

Skootum from Skotam meaning Trout.

SUNAPEE LAKE, N. H. This lake is situated on the west part of Merrimack County.

Sunapee from Sen'inebi meaning rock or mountain water.

Radical "sen'i" means of rock or mountain, "nebi" water.

SUNCOOK RIVER, N. H. This river rises near the summit of one Suncook Mountain, elevated 900 feet above its base.

Suncook from Sen'ikok meaning To the rocks.

Plural Nom:—Senal—*Rocks.*
　　　" 　Gen:—Sen'i—*Of the rocks.*
　　　" 　Dat:—Sen'ikok—*To the rocks.*

SOWADABSCOOK RIVER, ME. Penobscot Co. This stream falls into the Penobscot at Hampden, 5 miles below Bangor.

Sowadabscook from Sawadapskwok meaning To the jutting out rock.

Prefix "Sawa" means out, Suffif "Apskw" means rock.

Sawadapskw declined:

Nom:—Sawadapskw—*The sticking out rock.*
Gen:—Sawadapskw'i—*Of the sticking out rock.*
Dat:—Sawadapskw ok—*To the sticking out rock.*

SAUGATUCK RIVER. This river passes through Westport, it is hardly navigable to the village.

Saugatuck from Saagatekw meanig difficult to go up the river.

Prefix "Saaga" means hard or difficult, Suffix "tekw" means river.

SHAWSHEEN RIVER, Mass. This river rises in Lexington and Bedford and falls into the Merrimack at Andover, 20 miles N. by W. from Boston.

Shawsheen from Swassin for Joachim.

SEEKONK, Mass., Bristol Co. This town is watered by Seekonk or Pawtucket river. It lies 41 miles south from Boston.

Seekonk from Seg8nkw meaning skunk.

SCHOODIC Lakes and River, Me. These are large collections of water of very irregular form, lying principally in Washington County. Their outlet is a large stream of the same name.

Schoodic from Segodik meaning urine, on account of the colour and smell of the water.

SKUNGAMUG, Coventry, Conn., Tallan Co.

Skungamug from Sk8gamak meaning wide pond.

SKOWHEGAN, Me. Somerset Co. This town was formerly called Milburn. It took the Iidian name of the place in 1836. It is situated on the north side of the Kennebec river at Skowhegan Falls.

Skowhegan means the waiting and watching place of the Indians.

SHAMUT from Sam8d meaning giving them some food. It refers to the Indians giving some food to the first settlers at old Boston.

SEACONNET or Little Compton, R. I. Lies on the ocean, at the eastern entrance into Narraganset bay.

Seaconnet from Seguanek meaning A break-water.

— T —

TENAGA is the name of a place on the Gatineau River, about 15 miles from Ottawa.

Tenaga from Ktenaga.

Prefix "Kte" means great, sublime, romantic; Suffix "naga" means The shore or islands.

Ktenaga means It abounds in views of grand and romantic scenery.

TADOUSAC from Todosak meaning They pass or are passing by. The Indians usually stopped at Tadousac to sell their pelts, but some passed by going to Three Rivers.

Examples:—

Plural. N'dodosabna—*We pass by.*
K'dodosaba—*You pass by.*
Todasak—*They pass by.*

— U —

UNQUOWA, now Fairfield, Conn.

Unquowa from 8nkowa meaning To join together. It refers to the three parishes comprised in the town of Fairfield, viz. Green's Farms and Greenfield.

UNKATAQUISSIT, now Milton, Mass. Norfolk Co. This pleasant town lies 7 miles south from Boston, but by the granite bridge across the Neponset, the distance to the city is reduced to 6 miles.

Unkataquissit from 8nka taa kwassik meaning That is the very reason the distance is shorter.

Prefix "8nka" means the more or the less, "Taakwassik" means short.

UMBAGOG LAKE is a large body of water situated mostly in Maine.

Umbagog from W8mbagwog meaning To the clear water lake.

Prefix "W8m" means white, clear, Radical "Bagw means lake or pond and "og" to or from.

— W —

WONASQUATUCKET RIVER, R. I. Providence Co. This river rises in Smithfield and runs between North Providence and Johnton thus formins the head of Providence river.

Wonasquatucket from Wanaskwatekw meaning The head or source of a river.

Examples:—

Wanasquakwa means *The top or head of tree.*
Wanasquadna means *The head or summit of mountain.*

WSKANUSIGUA, Birch bark, peeled late in season but while there is some sap, is thick and hard. One strip of this bark, sufficient for one hunting canoe, is called "Wskanus igua" because it is nearly as hard as bone "Wskan".

WATCHAUG POND, in Charleston, Washington Co., R. I.

Watchaug from Wajok meaning At the mountain. It is supposed that the water there is as good as at the mountain.

WINICHAHANAT or Dover, N. H. This is one of the most interesting and important towns in New Hampshire. In the southern part of the town is a neck of land about two miles long and one-half mile broad, having Piscataqua on one side and Back river on the other. On this neck the first settlement was made nearly surrounded by water.

Winichahanat from Wiwnijoanek meaning literally. The place where the water flows around it.

WALLOOSTOOK RIVER, ME. This is the western or main branch of the St. John's river. Its head waters are in the counties of Somerset and Franklin and on the border of Canada.

Walloostook from Wallastekw meaning Shallow river.

Prefix "Wallas" means shallow, Suffix "tekw" means river.

WISCASSET, ME. Lincoln Co., is situated on the west side of Sheepscot river, 20 miles from the sea.

Wiscasset from Wikassit meaning Putting up buildings.

WATTUPPA PONDS, Mass. Fall River rises in Wattuppa ponds, one of which is 14 miles in length and one mile in breadth. These ponds are produced by perpetual springs.

Wattuppa from Wdopi meaning Alder.

WESSARANSET, Somerset Co., Me. This river is a branch of the Kennebec.

Wessaranset from Wass8lanset meaning Spearing.

WINOOSKI, Chittenden Co., Vt. This city is situated on both sides of Winooski river, one mile from Burlington Vt.

Winooski from Winuski meaning Onion land.

"Winus" means Onion, "ki" means land.

WINEPISAUKEE LAKE, N. H. This lake is situated in the County of Stratford.

Winepisaukee from Wiwninbes aki meaning Lake between and around land or islands.

Prefix "Wiwni" means around, Radical "nbes" means lake, Suffix "aki" means land or island.

WINNESIMET, ferry in old Boston.

Winnesimet from Wanesmid meaning drunk.

WONKINGUA RIVER, Mass.

Wonkingua from Wnegikw'i sibo meaning Otter river.

— Y —

Yamaska or Riviere des Savanes, a river of Quebec, takes its rise in Brome Lake and falls into the St. Lawrence at the head of Lake St. Peter.

YAMASKA from Ya Maska (sibo) meaning that is the Toad River.

Examples:—

Yo Alsig8ntekw—*This is the St. Francis River.*

Ni Ya Maska sibo—*And that is the Yamaska River.*

YAMACHICHE, river of Quebec, St. Maurice Co.

Yamachiche from Namashish meaning Small fish.

THE
ABREVIATED MANNER OF READING AND WRITING
IN ABENAKI

It is true that the words are long because they are a combination of two or three small words and these are composed of several two-letter syllables. It is easy to shorten the long words by using the following abreviations.

The letter "c" is used only before "h"
"g" is always hard.

A short horizontal line — under a letter, syllable or word means repetition as *"bis"*.

Examples:—

chi	for chi chi		mw	for miwi
da	" dada		mg	" m8gan
dz	" d8zo		ng	" nagw
dg	" d8gan		nk	" nakw
gm	" gamikw		n-g	" n8gw
gn	" gan		n-k	" n8kw
hg	" higan		nz	" n8zo
hz	" h8zo		ngn	" nigan
kn	" kan		tz	" t8zo
km	" kwan		wg	" w8gan
kg	" k8gan		wnn	" winno
l'	" hïa		wwz	" waw8wzo
mmk	" m8mek		zg	" zigan
mz	" migszo		zw	" ziwi

APPLICATION

Chibagi (ngz)	Chibagin8gwzo
Sogala (hg)	Sogalahigan
Ladaka (wg)	Ladakaw8gan
Wi (gwz) (wg)	Wig8wzow8gan
Chajig8 wi	Chajig8wiwi
Chi gu8gama	Chichigu8gama
Pizw8jmo (wg)	Pizw8jmow8gan
Wawig8 (dz)	Wawig8d8zo
Sal8kwa (zg)	Sal8kwazigan
Wli (ngz) (wg)	Wlin8gwzow8gan
W8leska (hg)	W8leskahigan
Kiwi (l') (wg)	Kiwihlaw8gan
Sazig8 (dz)	Sazig8dzo
Pazi (l') (wg)	Pazizihlaw8gan
Wlaka (mz) (wg)	Wlakamigzow8gan
La (kg)	Lak8gan
Pokwa	Popokwa
Ska (km)	Skakwan
Chita (hg)	Chitatahigan
Mam8lha (lk)	Mam8lhalokan
Naba (lk)	Nanabalokan
Mskag8dagi (l')	Mskag8dagihla
Sigosk8 (ng)	Sigosk8nigan
Sal8kwadi (gn)	Sal8kwadigan
8ji (tz)	8jit8zo
Sagiwi	Sasagiwi
Saskwa (wg)	Saskwaw8gan
Kwah8mo	Kwakwah8mo
M8liki (l')	M8likihla

Pawijo	Papawijo
Paga (mg)	Pagam8gan
Kita (dg)	Kitad8gan
Ka (ngn)	Kakanigan
Kika (wnn)	Kikawinno
Pka (l') gnigan	Pkahlagnigan
Adl8gwi	Adl8gwiwi
Aplesa (km)	Aplessakwam
Chawap (ngn)	Cawapnigan
Wl8mki (l')	Wl8mkihla
Aska (mw)	Askamiwi
Passo (jw)	Passojiwi
Sala (kw)	Salakiwi
Wl8gwi	Wl8gwiwi
Kaozi (gm)	Kaozigamikw
Skaskwat (sg)	Skaskwatsigan
Sipo (dg)	Sipodigan
Mdawa (wnn)	Mdawawinno
Wl8ma (wg)	Wl8maw8wgan
Wda (l') bika	Wdahlabika

MISS ALICE, THE AUTHOR'S DAUGHTER
Representing the Bouquet Girl
1911

BOUQUET PRESENTATION

The presentation of a bouquet to a young girl named Mary, on or about the 8th of December in commemoration of the salutation to the Virgin Mary was a custom of the Abenaki Indians which they semireligiously observer from time immemorial till three or four decades ago. If the bouquet was accepted by Mary's mother, then, presents in great number and variety were given to Mary. In return her parents gave a feast of venison: the flesh of moose and beaver and while justice is being done to this rare meal, the bouquet girl sings her song after which, every one present takes part in the dance called "Al8bagihl8mek" affording great enjoyment.

PSKWASAW8NI N8KSKWA

Awkiga mina lliwihlikakw Malgelit ala Madelan
  Pskwasaw8n'i N8kskwa ga ndeliwizi Pskwasaw8n aliwizia.

Akwiga toji kzalazikan ta8lawi wal8guiga
Knamiolop ki knamiolop adali nist8gwziakw wskinos
  Pskwasaw8n'i N8kskwa ga ndeliwizi Pskwasaw8n aliwizia.

Kaguiba nawa kizi idam nist8gwziaga wskinos
Ndeblodm8gonap ki nibaw8gan nitta ndali wli nkodmaw8n
  Pskwasaw8n'i N8kskwa ga ndeliwizi Pskwasaw8n aliwizia.

Psakwasaw8n ki yo pskwasaw8n nmessali waniad8gon
Nwaniad8gon nwaniad8gon n8nninska w8bi moniak
  Pskwasaw8n'i N8kskwa ga ndeliwizi Pskwasaw8n aliwizia.

N8damnn8guat pegua yo n8nninska w8bim8niak
Nwiag8wzow8gan waji m8joik ta nlaw8gan pmidwik
  Pskwasaw8n'i N8kskwa ga ndeliwizi Pskwasaw8n aliwizia.

BOUQUET GIRL

Call me not Marguerite or Madeleine any more
  I am Bouquet Girl since my name is Bouquet.

Be not so proud as last night
I saw you, yes saw you with a young man
  I am Bouquet Girl since my name is Bouquet.

What can you say against talking to a young man
He spoke to me about mariage and I answered agreeably
  I am Bouquet Girl since my name is Bouquet.

Bouquet this bouquet cost me a lot
It cost me fifty silver dollars
  I am Bouquet Girl since my name is Bouquet.

What is fifty silver dollars compared with
My pleasure and heart- strings
  I am Bouquet Girl since my name is Bouquet.

NID8BASSIS

Nid8bassis t8ni wadkannian?
Nd8biga achi nia nopawsa.   Kowanodana.
Nid8bassis t8ni nikw8bi?
Yugatta almadnassik nodossan.   Kowanodana
Nid8bassis kagwi padawian?
Nd8biga n8thebazi pot8ya.   Kowanodana.
Nid8bassis koji milessi?
Noz8mi tagastossi yudali.   Kowanodana.
Nid8bassis kzagin8gwzi.
Kiagata nimskam8ssi.   Kowanodana.
Nid8bassis ndaga t8m8 m8ni.
Aloka niji m8ni kwaj8nmen.   Kowanodana.
Nid8bassis ngini akwamalsi.
Kaguiji nawa kdelalokassi.   Kowanodana.
Nid8bassis n'8pchi machinassi.
Nid8ba s8gawiga kadosmi.   Kowanodana.

DEAR FRIEND

Dear friend where have you been traveling?
I also have been spotting,   Koanodana.
Dear friend where do you come from now?
From the mountain right here   Koanadana.
Dear friend what have you brought with you?
I went for a bottle and got it.   Koanodana.
Dear friend will you give me some?
I have none to spare here.   Koanodana.
Dear friend you are stingy.
Go for some yourself.   Koanodana.
Dear friend but I have no money.
Work and money you will have.   Koanodana.
Dear friend I am very sick.
What then can you do now?   Koanodana.
Dear friend I am dying.
Well then friend here have a drink.   Koanodana.